The Book of Job

The Book of Job

Kathleen M. O'Connor
with Little Rock Scripture Study staff

Little Rock Scripture Study

LITURGICAL PRESS
Collegeville, Minnesota

littlerockscripture.org

Nihil obstat for the commentary text by Kathleen M. O'Connor: Reverend Robert Harren, *Censor deputatus*.
Imprimatur for the commentary text by Kathleen M. O'Connor: ✠ Most Reverend John F. Kinney, J.C.D., D.D., Bishop of St. Cloud, Minnesota, October 12, 2012.

Cover design by John Vineyard. Interior art by Ned Bustard.

This symbol indicates material that was created by Little Rock Scripture Study to supplement the biblical text and commentary. Some of these inserts first appeared in the *Little Rock Catholic Study Bible*; others were created specifically for this book by Michael DiMassa.

Library of Congress Cataloging-in-Publication Data

Names: O'Connor, Kathleen M., 1942– author | Little Rock Scripture Study Staff author
Title: The book of Job / Kathleen M. O'Connor ; with Little Rock Scripture Study staff.
Description: Collegeville, Minnesota : Liturgical Press, [2026] | Series: Little Rock Scripture study | Summary: "Biblical scholar Kathleen O'Connor serves as an insightful guide in this exploration of the Book of Job. Commentary, study and reflection questions, prayers, and access to online lectures are included. 6 lessons"—Provided by publisher.
Identifiers: LCCN 2025029001 (print) | LCCN 2025029002 (ebook) | ISBN 9798400801297 trade paperback | ISBN 9798400801310 epub
Subjects: LCSH: Bible. Job—Study and teaching | Bible. Job—Commentaries
Classification: LCC BS1415.55 .O26 2026 (print) | LCC BS1415.55 (ebook)
LC record available at https://lccn.loc.gov/2025029001
LC ebook record available at https://lccn.loc.gov/2025029002

TABLE OF CONTENTS

Welcome	7
What materials will you use?	8
How will you use these materials?	8
Lesson One (Introduction and Job 1–3)	11
Lesson Two (Job 4–10)	27
Lesson Three (Job 11–19)	45
Lesson Four (Job 20–28)	63
Lesson Five (Job 29–37)	83
Lesson Six (Job 38–42)	103
Praying with Your Group	123
Reflecting on Scripture	125

Wrap-Up Lectures and Discussion Tips for Facilitators are available for each lesson at no charge. Find them online at LittleRockScripture.org/Lectures/Job.

Welcome

The Bible is at the heart of what it means to be a Christian. It is the Spirit-inspired word of God for us. It reveals to us the God who created, redeemed, and guides us still. It speaks to us personally and as a church. It forms the basis of our public liturgical life and our private prayer lives. It urges us to live worthily and justly, to love tenderly and wholeheartedly, and to be a part of building God's kingdom here on earth.

Though it was written a long time ago, in the context of a very different culture, the Bible is no relic of the past. Catholic biblical scholarship is among the best in the world, and in our time and place, we have unprecedented access to it. By making use of solid scholarship, we can discover much about the ancient culture and religious practices that shaped those who wrote the various books of the Bible. With these insights, and by praying with the words of Scripture, we allow the words and images to shape us as disciples. By sharing our journey of faithful listening to God's word with others, we have the opportunity to be stretched in our understanding and to form communities of love and learning. Ultimately, studying and praying with God's word deepens our relationship with Christ.

The Book of Job

The resource you hold in your hands is divided into six lessons. Each lesson involves personal prayer and study using this book and the experience of group prayer, discussion, and wrap-up lecture.

If you are using this resource in the context of a small group, we suggest that you meet six times, discussing one lesson per meeting. Allow about 90 minutes for the small group gathering. Small groups function best with eight to twelve people to ensure good group dynamics and to allow all to participate as they wish.

Some groups choose to have an initial gathering before their regular sessions begin. This allows an opportunity to meet one another, pass out books, and, if desired, view the optional intro lecture for this study available on the "Resources" page of the Little Rock Scripture Study website (littlerockscripture.org). Please note that there is only one intro lecture for two-part studies.

Every Bible study group is a little bit different. Some of our groups like to break each lesson up into two weeks of study so they are reading less each week and have more time to discuss the questions together at their weekly gatherings. If your group wishes to do this, simply agree how much of each lesson will be read each week, and only answer the questions that correspond to the material you read. Wrap-up lectures can then be viewed at the end of every other meeting rather than at the end of every meeting. Of course, this will mean that your study will last longer, and your group will meet more times.

WHAT MATERIALS WILL YOU USE?

The materials in this book include:

- The text of Job, using the New American Bible, Revised Edition as the translation.
- Commentary by Kathleen M. O'Connor (which has also been published separately as part of the New Collegeville Bible Commentary series).
- Occasional inserts highlighting elements of the chapters of Job being studied. Some of these appear also in the *Little Rock Catholic Study Bible* while others are supplied by staff writers.
- Questions for study, reflection, and discussion at the end of each lesson.
- Opening and closing prayers for each lesson, as well as other prayer forms available in the closing pages of the book.

In addition, there are wrap-up lectures available for each lesson. Your group may choose to purchase a DVD containing these lectures or make use of the video lectures available online at no charge. The link to these free lectures is: LittleRockScripture.org/Lectures/Job. Of course, if your group has access to qualified speakers, you may choose to have live presentations.

Each person will need a current translation of the Bible. We recommend the *Little Rock Catholic Study Bible*, which makes use of the New American Bible, Revised Edition. Other translations, such as the New Jerusalem Bible or the New Revised Standard Version: Catholic Edition, would also work well.

HOW WILL YOU USE THESE MATERIALS?

Prepare in advance

Using Lesson One as an example:

- Begin with a simple prayer like the one found on page 11.

- Read the assigned material for Lesson One (pages 12–21) so that you are prepared for the weekly small group session.
- Answer the questions, Exploring Lesson One, found at the end of the assigned reading, pages 22–24.
- Use the Closing Prayer on page 25 when you complete your study. This prayer may be used again when you meet with the group.

Meet with your small group

- After introductions and greetings, allow time for prayer (about 5 minutes) as you begin the group session. You may use the prayer on page 11 (also used by individuals in their preparation) or use a prayer of your choosing.
- Spend about 45–50 minutes discussing the responses to the questions that were prepared in advance. You may also develop your discussion further by responding to questions and interests that arise during the discussion and faith-sharing itself.
- Close the discussion and faith-sharing with prayer, about 5–10 minutes. You may use the Closing Prayer at the end of each lesson or one of your choosing at the end of the book. It is important to allow people to pray for personal and community needs and to give thanks for how God is moving in your lives.
- View the wrap-up lecture associated with each lesson (15–20 minutes). You may watch the lecture online, use a DVD, or provide a live lecture by a qualified local speaker. View the lecture together at the end of the session or, if your group runs out of time, you may invite group members to watch the lecture on their own time after the discussion.

A note to individuals

- If you are using this resource for individual study, simply move at your own pace. Take as much time as you need to read, study, and pray with the material.
- If you would like to share this experience with others, consider inviting a friend or family member to join you for your next study. Even a small group of two or three provides an opportunity for fruitful dialog and faith-sharing!

The Book of Job

LESSON ONE

Introduction and Job 1–3

Begin your personal study and group discussion with a simple and sincere prayer such as:

Prayer

Lord, grant that we may see your hand in every trial and triumph of our lives, knowing you are never absent from your people. May we remain steadfast in the belief that whatever our circumstances, you will never abandon us, for you are our rock and our salvation.

Read the Introduction on pages 12–13 and the Bible text of Job 1–3, found in the outside columns of pages 14–21, highlighting what stands out to you.

Read the accompanying commentary to add to your understanding.

Respond to the questions on pages 22–24, Exploring Lesson One.

The Closing Prayer on page 25 is for your personal use and may be used at the end of group discussion.

INTRODUCTION

The book of Job is vivid testimony to pain, a plea for justice, and a wrenching theological debate about suffering and its causes. Central to this debate are questions about the roles God and humans play in causing human suffering and whether divine-human relationship can proceed in the midst of overwhelming anguish. Like a riddle, the text grasps readers' minds and emotions, inviting them to participate in Job's story and to work toward their own solution to the dilemmas of both Job and his friends.

Literary features

The book's literary components do not fit easily together. It sets conflicting characters and discordant speeches side by side without providing interpretive clues. But rather than producing a mishmash of ideas, the resulting tensions summon readers to engage in Job's struggle, to stay with him on the ash heap and stand with him before God in search of healing. Because the book refuses to leave our present understandings intact, reading means undertaking mental and emotional labor. Job and his friends argue with each other in dense, beautiful poetic speeches, and they complain at length to wear the reader down. In the process, the poems bring us into Job's despair and his friends' frustration and growing rigidity.

But the effort required to read and study the book is worth it because the book's unsettled nature puts us either in Job's place or in sympathy with his friends or, perhaps, both. Precisely because it refuses to settle for easy answers about any of its subjects, the book of Job is a classic of world literature.

Most interpreters believe the book as we now have it is a composite, built upon an ancient tale about an innocent sufferer. The outlines of Job's story were well-known across cultures in antiquity. Peoples of the ancient Near East produced several texts with affinities to the biblical book where an innocent person undergoes suffering, argues with the gods, and is inexplicably restored to well-being. Job also appears by name in a biblical list of heroes (Ezek 14:14, 20), adding to the sense that his basic story was widely known.

It is likely that a writer in ancient Israel took this folktale, adapted it, cut it open, and then set the poetic speeches in the midst of it. The prose narrative appears in the prologue (1:1–2:13) and epilogue (42:7-17). By using both forms of literature, folktale and poetry, the book presents a totality of suffering, an overwhelming portrait told from outside by a third person narrator in the prose and from the inside in the poetic testimony of Job and his friends. The prose describes Job's external losses, while the poetry portrays Job's more internal sufferings.

Poetry is particularly suited to the task of spiritual struggle because its dense imagery, compactness of speech, and allusiveness create an artistic world something like music. It appeals to the full humanity of readers, summoning forth our own ghosts, unsettled sorrows, and hidden angers. It can transport us into realms of spirit and lead to new discoveries. But the poetry of Job makes best sense when read in the context of the prose narrative that lays out the book's initial problem. Job is an innocent person yet enormous catastrophes befall him because of a deal made in heaven. This predicament gives rise to the poetry.

The prose and the poetry belong together, but there are great differences between them. In the prologue, for example, Job is patient and trusting while his friends are silent. By contrast, in the poetry Job is furious and impatient and his friends flood him with words. This is one of the many gaps that raise questions about characters and their motivations, thereby engaging us in Job's plight.

Job's poetry uses a great deal of legal imagery as a way for Job to imagine that God might acknowledge his innocence. Job appeals to a third party to assist him in his search for justice because his informal appeals to God seem to produce nothing but more sorrow. He declares legal oaths of innocence by which he offers his self-defense at the end of his speeches. But legal language is only one way Job voices his complaints. Language of creation and observations from the world of plants and animals help him build his protests.

Much of Job's speech takes the form of lamentation. Over one third of the book of Psalms and the entire book of Lamentations are laments. These are prayers in the form of complaint. The one who prays cries out to God in pain, describes various forms of affliction, and seeks redress. Laments are a form of truth-telling to God. They open up rather than deny suffering, and they present to God the affliction of the one who prays and demands action. In Old Testament laments, anger at God and fury close to blasphemy are instruments of fidelity because they keep the relationship with God alive in the midst of suffering. They are acts of faith that God cares for the afflicted and can bear to hear the truth. By using laments, Job grows strong and courageous as he clings to God under the worst conditions.

Wisdom literature

The book of Job belongs in a grouping of biblical books called the wisdom literature that includes Proverbs, Ecclesiastes, Sirach, and the Wisdom of Solomon. These books differ from other biblical literature in their attention to daily struggles of ordinary human life. By contrast, the prophetic books speak of God's word to the people, and the historical books tell of God's actions on behalf of Israel. Wisdom starts neither with God nor with large political and national events, but from human efforts to live wisely from day to day. Life's challenges give rise to theological reflection, not the other way around. Job is merely going on with his daily life when disasters overtake him, and those events propel his theological questions. In wisdom thinking, at least in the book of Proverbs, faithful living should yield material blessing. When Job loses everything, his fidelity to God is suspect.

Job's cultural world

Job lived in a different cultural world from that of contemporary Western readers, though people in tribal communities on various continents may find many affinities with aspects of the book. Job lived in a community-oriented culture. The family and clan were of high value, and one sought to become wise and learn proverbs in order to create harmony for the community, not for self-advancement as in individual-oriented cultures.

Israel's culture as reflected in wisdom literature was deeply concerned about the authenticity of speech, about proper use of the tongue, and about wise sayings or proverbs as a key to right behavior. Proverbs are short sayings that were instruments of wise living and the storehouse of tradition. Because the culture was an oral one, the right use of words was critical for communal well-being. Wisdom drawn from animal and plant life instructed humans in how to maneuver in daily life and how to contribute to the community. Both Job and his friends apply proverbs to his situation, but their proverbs usually conflict with one another.

Other features of ancient Israel's culture important for understanding the book include the values of honor and shame. Shame was a communal judgment, often implicit, that one's behavior or attitude brought dishonor to the community. To be shamed means one has been disrespectful of persons or basic values in the community. Job begins the story as a most honorable person, but his disasters cause him shame and isolation from his friends. He loses his good name and his community no longer recognizes his honor, isolating him and causing him great anguish.

Outline of the book

The book divides into the following literary units:

The Prologue (1:1–2:13)
Three Rounds of Speeches among Job and His Friends (3:1–14:22; 15:1–21:34; 22:1–31:40)
Hymn to Wisdom (28:1-28)
Job's Self-Defense (29:1–31:40)
Elihu's Speeches (32:1–37:24)
The Encounter with God in the Storm (38:1–42:6)
The Epilogue (42:7-17)

I: Prologue

CHAPTER 1

Job's Piety

1 In the land of Uz there was a blameless and
upright man named Job, who feared God and
avoided evil. 2 Seven sons and three daughters were
born to him; 3 and he had seven thousand sheep,
three thousand camels, five hundred yoke of oxen,
five hundred she-donkeys, and a very large household, so that he was greater than anyone in the
East. 4 His sons used to take turns giving feasts,
sending invitations to their three sisters to eat and
drink with them. 5 And when each feast had run
its course, Job would send for them and sanctify them, rising early and offering sacrifices for every one of them. For Job said, "It may be that my children have sinned and cursed God in their hearts." Job did this habitually.

continue

PROLOGUE

Job 1:1–2:13

The prose prologue begins with a depiction of a contented Job, residing in security, wealth, and domestic tranquility. A narrator describes events that move through the slow but complete unraveling of these good things and end in grief on the ash heap. Events alternate in the five scenes between earth and heaven; events in heaven determine what happens on earth. The narrative unfolds in highly stylized fashion with sparse detail and repeated patterns typical of a folktale. The effects of this narrative style are to present a hammering sequence of events that shatters Job's world and leaves many unanswered questions about divine and human characters and their motivations.

1:1-5 Job's goodness

The opening scene takes place on earth where every detail contributes to a portrait of Job as an innocent man, beloved of God. The narrator calls him "blameless and upright," one who "feared God," and "avoided evil" (1:1). To "fear God" is a common term of the wisdom literature that has less to do with fright before God and more to do with right relationship with God. "Fear of God" is not easy to translate into English but conveys qualities of obedience, reverence, and awe before God. One commentator calls it a synonym for true religion. Job's fear of God marks him as a wise and righteous man. His large family and vast wealth in animal holdings confirm his blamelessness and special relationship with God. In antiquity, material wealth signified that its bearer was a worthy recipient of divine favor.

Job's uprightness receives further confirmation from the size of his family and the peaceful generosity of his children. His seven sons invite his three daughters to their feasts, showing their hospitality to exceed the bounds of their culture where women had little status. And perhaps most indicative of Job's righteousness is a detail in which he exceeds all obvious requirements of care for his family by offering sacrifice on behalf of his children in case they have sinned "in their hearts" (1:5). In its spare telling, the story leaves readers to ponder Job's behavior. Is he an overly scrupulous parent? Does he act to protect the children? Or is this one more instance of his absolute devotion to God? The folktale genre of the prologue, however, may preclude suspicions about Job's character, for folktales typically tell actions as straightforward events to be taken at face value. The next scenes support the view that fidelity alone motivates Job.

1:6-12 Deal in heaven

The action starts when messengers, called "sons of God," come before "the LORD" in the heavenly court. Heavenly courts with semi-divine beings of the spirit world appear elsewhere in the Old Testament (1 Kgs 22:19-23; Dan 7). Among the heavenly messengers is "the satan," whose name means "the adversary," an official court title, not a proper name. He is not yet the demonic figure of later Jewish and Christian thinking, but one of the Lord's faithful servants, though it is easy to see from his role here how he might later come to personify evil.

The Lord starts the action by asking the satan if, when traveling to and fro on the earth, he had noticed "my servant Job" (1:8). Should

The Interview Between the Lord and the Satan

6One day, when the sons of God came to present themselves before the LORD, the satan also came among them. 7The LORD said to the satan, "Where have you been?" Then the satan answered the LORD and said, "Roaming the earth and patrolling it." 8The LORD said to the satan, "Have you noticed my servant Job? There is no one on earth like him, blameless and upright, fearing God and avoiding evil." 9The satan answered the LORD and said, "Is it for nothing that Job is God-fearing? 10Have you not surrounded him and his family and all that he has with your protection? You have blessed the work of his hands, and his livestock are spread over the land. 11But now put forth your hand and touch all that he has, and surely he will curse you to your face." 12The LORD said to the satan, "Very well, all that he has is in your power;

continue

Who Is Satan?

Originally, "Satan" was not what Christians understand as the devil. Rather, it was any opponent, human or heavenly. The Hebrew word *satan* simply means "adversary." Several of Solomon's political opponents are referred to as *satan* in the original Hebrew text (1 Kgs 11:14, 23, 25). When Balaam sets out to curse (or bless) the Israelites, the angel of the Lord stands in his way as a *satan* to stop him (Num 22:22, 32).

In books of the Old Testament that were written later, the *satan* often acts as a kind of prosecuting attorney, pointing out human failings to God and testing their fidelity. In First Chronicles a *satan* lures David into taking a census (21:1). The high priest Joshua, who symbolically bears the sins of the people, is accused by a *satan* standing at the Lord's right hand (Zech 3:1-5). The *satan* who appears in the book of Job has this same function. He is a member of God's divine council, one of the "sons of God" (later considered to be angels). He defends God's rights, pointing out that Job may be taking advantage of God, and is given permission to test Job's virtue.

The understanding of a *satan* as an opponent and accuser of human beings forms the foundation of the New Testament figure of Satan. In the New Testament Satan is no longer defending God but rather is attempting to separate people from God through temptation and deceit. Even Jesus is tempted by Satan (Mark 1:13). The earlier understanding of the word *satan* as an opponent does appear, however, when Peter attempts to convince Jesus that he will not suffer and die. Jesus says, "Get behind me, Satan. You are thinking not as God does, but as human beings do" (Mark 8:33).

In the New Testament the figure of evil called Satan is also termed the "devil," a word derived from the Greek translation of *satan*, which is *diabolos*.

only do not lay a hand on him." So the satan went
forth from the presence of the LORD.

The First Trial

[13]One day, while his sons and daughters were
eating and drinking wine in the house of their el-
dest brother, [14]a messenger came to Job and said,
"The oxen were plowing and the donkeys grazing
beside them, [15]and the Sabeans carried them off in
a raid. They put the servants to the sword, and I
alone have escaped to tell you." [16]He was still
speaking when another came and said, "God's fire
has fallen from heaven and struck the sheep and
the servants and consumed them; I alone have
escaped to tell you." [17]He was still speaking when
another came and said, "The Chaldeans formed
three columns, seized the camels, carried them off,
and put the servants to the sword; I alone have
escaped to tell you." [18]He was still speaking when
another came and said, "Your sons and daughters
were eating and drinking wine in the house of their
eldest brother, [19]and suddenly a great wind came
from across the desert and smashed the four cor-
ners of the house. It fell upon the young people
and they are dead; I alone have escaped to tell you."

Job's Reaction

[20]Then Job arose and tore his cloak and cut off
his hair. He fell to the ground and worshiped.
[21]He said,

"Naked I came forth from my mother's womb,
and naked shall I go back there.
The LORD gave and the LORD has taken away;
blessed be the name of the LORD!"

[22]In all this Job did not sin, nor did he charge
God with wrong.

continue

readers still question Job's innocence, God's authoritative boasting repeats the narrator's assessment of Job's innocence. Job is "blameless and upright, fearing God and avoiding evil" (1:8). The satan, however, suspects Job is faithful only because God has given him good things. He accuses God of purchasing Job's fidelity, for if God were to remove them, "surely [Job] will curse you to your face" (1:11). The Hebrew word translated "curse" means literally "to bless," but here "bless" is a euphemism, that is, a polite way to say the opposite.

Without hesitation and without debate, the Lord gives the satan control of Job's life with one caveat—he is not to touch Job. Why God acquiesces to this deal is not clear. It may be that refusing the satan's challenge would cause God shame in this ancient Israelite culture where honor is of high value. Or it may be that God is so confident of Job's loyalty that a positive outcome of the deal seems assured. Whatever God's reasons for abdicating power, the satan goes forth to loose tragedy upon Job.

1:13-22 Job's first test

Back on earth, catastrophes roll over Job in quick succession. In simple, unadorned prose, the story unfolds in parallel episodes so each disaster appears like the one before in a persistent drumbeat of loss. Events concerning Job's children form a literary frame around his other losses (1:13, 18-19). By setting the other disasters during one of their feasts, the text creates a foreboding sense of doom and foreshadows the fourth and most horrible of Job's devastations. A messenger comes to announce each tragedy and says, "I alone have escaped to tell you" (1:15, 16, 17, 18). And "He was still speaking when" the next messenger appears with a similar report. Finally, in the horrible climax, the narrator gives extra description to the children's destruction. A great wind destroys the house where they are feasting and kills all of them. Within a few verses, Job loses everything in a whirlwind of calamity, a blitz of overwhelmingly bad news.

To this point in the telling, Job has made no response to any of the reports, but then in customary rituals for expressing grief, he tears his clothes, cuts his hair, and falls upon the ground. At last he speaks in carefully balanced sentences typical of Hebrew poetry. "Naked I came forth . . . naked shall I go back . . . The LORD gave

. . . the LORD has taken away" (1:21). Then he blesses God's name. Job does not curse God and the narrator confirms that Job does not "sin, nor did he charge God with wrong" (1:22).

2:1-6 Another bad deal in heaven

The story might have ended in the previous chapter where, even in the aftermath of the unrelenting assault upon him, Job proved himself blameless and upright, a God-fearer, and a refuser of evil. Instead, when the heavenly messengers come before the Lord again, the tension escalates. The narrative follows the first heavenly scene of the previous chapter, but with some important changes. Again God asks the satan where he has been and if he has seen his "servant Job" who remains "blameless and upright, fearing God and avoiding evil" (2:3). In still a further affirmation of Job, God accuses the satan of manipulation in order to harm Job without cause.

The satan replies "skin for skin," a short saying that probably means, if you harm someone's skin, they will harm yours in turn. His principle of human behavior is that people may remain faithful when you take their things or their loved ones, but if you attack their bodies and threaten their lives, they will do anything. The satan applies his principle to Job, insisting that Job will "curse you to your face" (2:5). Again without explanation, God relinquishes Job into the satan's power. The only constraint on the satan is that he preserve Job's life.

CHAPTER 2

The Second Interview

1One day, when the sons of God came to
present themselves before the LORD, the satan also
came with them. 2The LORD said to the satan,
"Where have you been?" Then the satan answered
the LORD and said, "Roaming the earth and pa-
trolling it." 3The LORD said to the satan, "Have you
noticed my servant Job? There is no one on earth
like him, blameless and upright, fearing God and
avoiding evil. He still holds fast to his innocence
although you incited me against him to ruin him
for nothing." 4The satan answered the LORD and
said, "Skin for skin! All that a man has he will give
for his life. 5But put forth your hand and touch his
bone and his flesh. Then surely he will curse you
to your face." 6And the LORD said to the satan, "He
is in your power; only spare his life."

continue

The first two chapters of Job are carefully structured in **five alternating scenes** that introduce the main characters and describe the onset of Job's suffering.

	Place	Characters	Content
Scene 1 (1:1-5)	Job's house	Job; his children	Job's wealth and goodness
Scene 2 (1:6-12)	God's court	God; the divine council ("sons of God") including the satan	God's boast; the satan's challenge; God's permission to afflict Job
Scene 3 (1:13-22)	Job's house	Job; his children and servants	Job's loss of family and property; his acceptance
Scene 4 (2:1-6)	God's court	God; the divine council; the satan	Renewal of God's boast and the satan's challenge; God's permission to destroy Job's health
Scene 5 (2:7-13)	Job's house	Job and his wife; his friends	Job's loss of health; his wife's challenge; his acceptance; the friends' sympathy

The Second Trial

7So the satan went forth from the presence of
the LORD and struck Job with severe boils from
the soles of his feet to the crown of his head.

Job's Reaction

8He took a potsherd to scrape himself, as he
sat among the ashes. 9Then his wife said to him,
"Are you still holding to your innocence? Curse
God and die!" 10But he said to her, "You speak as
foolish women do. We accept good things from
God; should we not accept evil?" Through all this,
Job did not sin in what he said.

Job's Three Friends

11Now when three of Job's friends heard of all
the misfortune that had come upon him, they set
out each one from his own place: Eliphaz from
Teman, Bildad from Shuh, and Zophar from Naa-
math. They met and journeyed together to give
him sympathy and comfort. 12But when, at a dis-
tance, they lifted up their eyes and did not recog-
nize him, they began to weep aloud; they tore
their cloaks and threw dust into the air over their

continue

2:7-10 Job's second test

The satan goes forth again and afflicts Job with severe boils that cover his body. To convey the horror of Job's physical condition, the narrator mentions the simple detail of a potsherd, a piece of broken pottery Job uses for wound-scraping as he sits on the ash heap (2:8). Job's nameless wife appears only in this scene, but her question intones a theme of both the prologue and the book. "Are you still holding to your innocence?" she asks. The Hebrew word translated "innocence" also means "integrity" or "wholeness" in the sense of deeply held honesty and blamelessness.

Job's wife's motivations have provoked debate among interpreters. When she advises him to curse God and die, is she betraying him? In the ancient world, people believed cursing God brought certain death. Does his wife want him to die because she cannot bear to see him suffer? Or is her question a literary device to provoke Job's response? Everything comes from God, he proclaims, so should we not accept both good and evil? Job has passed the second test in patient fidelity.

2:11-13 The friends

Job's three friends hear of his tragedy and travel to see him, but they do not recognize him, so altered is he by his suffering. So

Job's Comforters (2:12), William Blake

Job's Wife

Job's suffering is well known to us, but his wife (who is not named) surely suffered as well. Not only did she lose her children and see the decay of the land and cattle that had supported them, but she lost her husband for a while as well. He was lost to her in his mourning and in his reasoning and questioning.

The only mention of Job's wife in this story demonstrates her bitterness, her hopelessness, and even her lack of faith in a God who would torture her husband in this way. "Curse God and die!" (2:9) is her way of saying to him: either you are to blame for this, or everything you believe about God is false; there's nothing to be gained from hanging on to your beliefs. Perhaps she helped Job to struggle even more honestly with the God he loved and in whom he trusted.

Was the faith of Job's wife restored as time wore on and Job came to an even more confident faith that continued to believe in God's creative and regenerative power? Or did she become disillusioned and angry? The only thing we know for sure is that God restored Job in unexpected and extravagant ways. Surely part of this restoration included his relationship with his wife.

stunned are they, they can find no words adequate to comfort him. They lament, tear their clothes, and put dust on their heads according to ancient mourning rituals. For a week they sit with him, mercifully silent, and perhaps numbed themselves, companions who see "how great was his suffering" (2:13). Their silent companionship may be their deepest act of friendship.

FIRST ROUND OF SPEECHES

Job 3:1–14:22

To cross from the prose prologue into the poetry in the book is to move into an altered world. Job is no longer the "patient man" of popular opinion but an enraged, impatient, and broken human. His friends, provoked by his outburst in chapter 3, also break their silence and offer advice to comfort and guide him into their version of the "truth"of his situation. Job's suffering expands in the poetic speeches for they add to his suffering internal anguish that compounds his pain. His friends fail to understand him and cannot relinquish their belief that he must be guilty of sin and so he must have caused his own suffering. Job himself has no other explanation for his

heads. 13 Then they sat down upon the ground
with him seven days and seven nights, but none
of them spoke a word to him; for they saw how
great was his suffering.

II. First Cycle of Speeches

CHAPTER 3

Job's Complaint

1 After this, Job opened his mouth and cursed
his day. 2 Job spoke out and said:

3 Perish the day on which I was born,
 the night when they said, "The child is
  a boy!"
4 May that day be darkness:
 may God above not care for it,
 may light not shine upon it!
5 May darkness and gloom claim it,
 clouds settle upon it,
 blackness of day affright it!
6 May obscurity seize that night;
 may it not be counted among the days of
  the year,
 nor enter into the number of the months!

continue

[7]May that night be barren;
let no joyful outcry greet it!
[8]Let them curse it who curse the Sea,
those skilled at disturbing Leviathan!
[9]May the stars of its twilight be darkened;
may it look for daylight, but have none,
nor gaze on the eyes of the dawn,
[10]Because it did not keep shut the doors of
the womb
to shield my eyes from trouble!
[11]Why did I not die at birth,
come forth from the womb and expire?
[12]Why did knees receive me,
or breasts nurse me?
[13]For then I should have lain down and been
tranquil;
had I slept, I should then have been at rest
[14]With kings and counselors of the earth
who rebuilt what were ruins
[15]Or with princes who had gold
and filled their houses with silver.
[16]Or why was I not buried away like a
stillborn child,
like babies that have never seen the light?
[17]There the wicked cease from troubling,
there the weary are at rest.

continue

overwhelming misery than that God has betrayed him. Together the speeches of Job and his friends offer conflicting interpretations of Job's suffering without indicating which one might be correct. This mode of theological debate encourages readers to weigh each view and to come to terms with the drama of Job's life themselves and perhaps also with the suffering within and around them.

3:1-10 Job curses his birth

Job curses both the day of his birth (3:1-6) and the night of his conception (3:7-10), two continuous moments in the creation of his life. His curse is actually a series of wishes, impossible appeals, not only to undo his life but also to unmake, to cancel out God's creation of his birthday. As a way to develop dramatic tension, the poem withholds the reason for his curse until verse ten. Prior to that, Job presents his suffering as part of the larger cosmic battle between light and darkness, order and chaos, life and death. Upon the day of his birth, he heaps a series of synonyms for darkness. He wishes to obliterate his day of birth from the calendar, as if it were possible to reach back in time and blot out his life from human history. Job wants to turn the day of his birth, normally a time of joy, into empty gloom. Daylight should turn to darkness, no light should shine, darkness should claim his day, and the dark night itself should frighten the day from even existing.

When Job steps back further in time to the night of his conception, he wishes to destroy the joyful night of his parents' lovemaking and the beginning of his life in the womb (3:7-10). Underlying his curse of the night are ancient Canaanite myths in which chaos struggles with order and life with death. Chaos was represented as the sea and sometimes as a mythic sea monster, here called "Leviathan" (3:8). Job desperately seeks a mysterious group of people who are able to raise up Leviathan to help him curse his conception. The poem poetically turns the night into a person who cannot find the morning light or gaze at the "eyes of the dawn" (3:9). The climax of the poem comes when Job finally proclaims the reason for his curses—the night did not shut the door to his mother's womb (3:10). Had he never been born or conceived, he would not have to face his present troubles.

3:11-19 Job's despair

Job elaborates on his desire never to have been born with a series of questions about his birth (3:11-12). Since his conception was unavoidable, he would rather have been a stillborn or an abandoned infant with no one to nurse him. Then death would have come quickly, and he would be at rest rather than living in turmoil and pain. Death attracts him because it is a state of rest, free of pain. He imagines the world of the dead as a place occupied by many elite people who, in a democracy of the underworld, rest together with captives and slaves. In death everyone is free from oppression and from distinctions of class. Small and great are the same. To be there is better than to be alive in misery.

3:20-26 Why does anyone suffer?

Job's suffering expands his imagination and compassion. He moves in his mind from the world of the dead to the plight of other suffering people. His afflictions lead him to wonder why anyone suffers, why anyone would know so much anguish to make them long for death and to desire the grave. Job's sudden and colossal misery enables the once rich, powerful man to see beyond his own world to the larger torments of others. In Job's view, the reason people suffer is because God "hems" them in (3:23). Job sighs and groans and has discovered that he has little control over anything. Death is preferable because in death there is rest.

18The captives are at ease together,
and hear no overseer's voice.
19Small and great are there;
the servant is free from the master.
20Why is light given to the toilers,
life to the bitter in spirit?
21They wait for death and it does not come;
they search for it more than for hidden
treasures.
22They rejoice in it exultingly,
and are glad when they find the grave:
23A man whose path is hidden from him,
one whom God has hemmed in!
24For to me sighing comes more readily
than food;
my groans well forth like water.
25For what I feared overtakes me;
what I dreaded comes upon me.
26I have no peace nor ease;
I have no rest, for trouble has come!

What Is Sheol?

In ancient Israel, belief in life after death was limited. It was believed that everyone—good and bad—went to a place called Sheol (a Hebrew word that is sometimes translated as "netherworld" or "underworld"). Existence in Sheol was little better than suspended animation. There was no pain, no joy, no memory, no communication, no light. Sometimes it is assumed that God is not present in Sheol (e.g., Ps 88:11-13), but elsewhere the psalmist asserts, "[I]f I lie down in Sheol, there you are" (139:8). Although Job does not use the word "Sheol" in chapter 3, he gives a good description of it (3:13-19).

When belief in the resurrection of the dead began to develop in the mid-second century BCE, Sheol came to be seen as a place of punishment for the wicked, what we now call "hell." In the New Testament, Hades (the Greek word for Sheol or netherworld) sometimes connotes death or hell (see Matt 11:23; 16:18; Luke 10:15; 16:23; Acts 2:27, 31) and sometimes seems to be a temporary place for the dead before the Last Judgment (Rev 20:13-14).

EXPLORING LESSON ONE

1. a) What were your impressions of the book of Job before you began to study it?

   b) What questions do you have about human suffering? What do you hope to gain from your study of Job?

2. What is the relationship between prose and poetry in the book of Job? Why is poetry a helpful genre for dealing with difficult human questions and experiences?

3. What is a lament, and what is the benefit of this type of prayer in one's relationship with God? (See Ps 69 for another example.)

4. Describe one aspect of Job's culture that is important for understanding the book of Job.

5. a) What kind of man is Job (1:1-5)?

   b) What is the significance of Job's wealth? (See also Gen 13:2; Deut 28:1-14.)

6. Who is "the satan," and how is this figure different from the demonic figure we call "Satan" today (1:6-12)?

7. Job's loss is enormous, as is his grief (1:13-22; 2:7-10). Reflect on a time when you have suffered great loss. What were some of your reactions? How did you pray after your loss?

8. Reflect on the initial encounter of Job with his three friends (2:11-13). When have friends accompanied you in times of loss or grief? What did they say or do (or *not* say or do) that was most meaningful or helpful?

9. How does the characterization of Job change as the text moves from prose (1:1–2:13) to poetry (3:1-26)?

10. What strikes you most about Job's first complaint (3:1-26)? Do you relate to anything in particular that Job says?

CLOSING PRAYER

"Naked I came forth from my mother's womb,
and naked shall I go back there.
The Lord *gave and the* Lord *has taken away;*
blessed be the name of the Lord*!"* (Job 1:21)

Heavenly Father, we pray for the grace to accept with tranquility the suffering that inevitably comes into our lives. Trusting in your great love and firm in the belief that all things are working toward our good (Rom 8:28), may we find joy in the good things in our lives and not despair at their loss. We pray today for all those who are suffering the loss of health, employment, loved ones, or peace of mind, especially . . .

LESSON TWO

Job 4–10

Begin your personal study and group discussion with a simple and sincere prayer such as:

Lord, grant that we may see your hand in every trial and triumph of our lives, knowing you are never absent from your people. May we remain steadfast in the belief that whatever our circumstances, you will never abandon us, for you are our rock and our salvation.

Read the Bible text of Job 4–10, found in the outside columns of pages 28–39, highlighting what stands out to you.

Read the accompanying commentary to add to your understanding.

Respond to the questions on pages 40–42, Exploring Lesson Two.

The Closing Prayer on page 43 is for your personal use and may be used at the end of group discussion.

CHAPTER 4

Eliphaz's First Speech

1Then Eliphaz the Temanite answered and said:

2If someone attempts a word with you,
would you mind?
How can anyone refrain from speaking?
3Look, you have instructed many,
and made firm their feeble hands.
4Your words have upheld the stumbler;
you have strengthened faltering knees.
5But now that it comes to you, you are
impatient;
when it touches you, you are dismayed.
6Is not your piety a source of confidence,
and your integrity of life your hope?
7Reflect now, what innocent person perishes?
Where are the upright destroyed?
8As I see it, those who plow mischief
and sow trouble will reap them.
9By the breath of God they perish,
and by the blast of his wrath they are
consumed.
10Though the lion roars, though the king of
beasts cries out,
yet the teeth of the young lions are broken;
11The old lion perishes for lack of prey,
and the cubs of the lioness are scattered.
12A word was stealthily brought to me,
my ear caught a whisper of it.

continue

4:1–5:27 Eliphaz's first speech

Eliphaz from Teman is the most gentle of Job's three friends, all of whom are deeply rooted in the theology that people bring suffering upon themselves. Often called the "theology of retribution," the thinking is that if you do good things, you receive good things in return, and vice versa. Across the book, Job's friends will defend this view and interpret Job's life through it. But no matter their theology, the three friends care deeply for Job and wish to see him released from his suffering.

Respectfully, Eliphaz asks Job if he is willing to hear, if he is open to wise counsel. Implying that Job was once a vocal proponent of the theology of his friends, Eliphaz reminds him of his past support of people who faltered along life's journey (4:3-4). Now Job must preach to himself. With a rhetorical question, Eliphaz goes to the heart of the theology Job once shared with these friends (4:7). In his view, the innocent and the upright do not perish. Instead, they are safe and therefore Job can face the future in confidence.

Using a style of argument typical of wisdom literature, Eliphaz contrasts the fate of the innocent with the fate of troublemakers (4:8-11). "Those who plow mischief" will get what they deserve, because God's angry breath will destroy them. The moral dynamic is clear; humans determine their own fate and Job must choose which group, the innocent or the wicked, he wishes to be among. And again using a common speech form of wisdom, Eliphaz speaks in proverb-like sayings that draw wisdom from the animal and plant world. His reference to lions is not connected grammatically to the fate of the wicked, but it probably means that even these powerful beasts have to put up with travail and loss, so Job should expect no less.

Eliphaz claims that theological authority for his advice comes from his experience of "visions of the night," a dream-like revelation experienced by him alone (4:12-21). A spirit visits, frightens, and questions him, and then answers the questions. All creatures are sinful before God, even heavenly beings. Humans, made only of clay and dust, are even more sinful than corrupt denizens of the spirit world. Humans die and may never learn wisdom, presumably the wisdom of their true sinful condition. Depicting the fragility of human life, the visiting spirit speaks of human bodies as houses and tents, temporary dwellings that crush, shatter, or pluck up easily (4:19-21). That life is fragile and humans sinful should be a warning to Job.

Eliphaz's advice grows less gentle when he points to Job's isolation in his suffering (5:1-2). There are no holy ones to whom Job might appeal for help. Whereas some interpreters believe Eliphaz's claim about holy ones is a putdown of ancient beliefs in lesser gods who

13In my thoughts during visions of the night,
when deep sleep falls on mortals,
14Fear came upon me, and shuddering,
that terrified me to the bone.
15Then a spirit passed before me,
and the hair of my body stood on end.
16It paused, but its likeness I could not
recognize;
a figure was before my eyes,
in silence I heard a voice:
17"Can anyone be more in the right than God?
Can mortals be more blameless than their
Maker?
18Look, he puts no trust in his servants,
and even with his messengers he finds fault.
19How much more with those who dwell in
houses of clay,
whose foundation is in the dust,
who are crushed more easily than a moth!

continue

Job's Three Friends

When his family is wiped out and his property is utterly destroyed, Job sinks into despair, suffering from a hideous skin disease. The book of Job describes Job's losses, his reflections on loss, his despairing arguments with God, and—finally—his submission to God's greatness and power. Through it all, Job is accompanied by three "friends."

Eliphaz, Bildad, and Zophar travel "to give [Job] sympathy and comfort" (2:11). They weep, rend their garments, and throw dust on their heads (all signs of mourning), and then sit with Job for seven days and nights. The text is clear that the friends do nothing but sit with him during this time—they do not speak "a word" because words could not begin to ease his suffering (2:13).

Perhaps their silent vigil does not last long enough. When Job begins to lament his own existence and search for answers to explain his suffering, the friends are more than willing to supply answers. In a series of speeches (chapters 4–25), each of Job's friends attempts to explain his suffering by using timeworn explanations: perhaps Job is reaping the harvest of his own sin; perhaps he is suffering God's judgment; or perhaps he is even a victim of his own self-righteousness.

The book of Job is an attempt to wrestle with the reality that even good people suffer. It is a recognition that the world does not always operate on a logical system of cause and effect, and that traditional thinking cannot penetrate the mystery of human suffering. Job's friends may not have been the best at offering sympathy, but they serve a literary purpose—their arguments move the story forward. They offer Job the opportunity to punch holes in the traditional belief that suffering is connected to sinfulness.

[20]Morning or evening they may be shattered;
unnoticed, they perish forever.
[21]The pegs of their tent are plucked up;
they die without knowing wisdom."

CHAPTER 5

[1]Call now! Will anyone respond to you?
To which of the holy ones will you turn?
[2]Surely impatience kills the fool
and indignation slays the simpleton.
[3]I have seen a fool spreading his roots,
but I cursed his household suddenly:
[4]May his children be far from safety;
may they be crushed at the gate without a rescuer.
[5]What they have reaped may the hungry eat up,
or God take away by blight,
or the thirsty swallow their substance.
[6]For not from dust does mischief come,
nor from the soil does trouble sprout.
[7]Human beings beget mischief
as sparks fly upward.
[8]In your place, I would appeal to God,
and to God I would state my plea.
[9]He does things great and unsearchable,
things marvelous and innumerable.
[10]He gives rain upon the earth
and sends water upon the fields;
[11]He sets up the lowly on high,
and those who mourn are raised to safety.
[12]He frustrates the plans of the cunning,
so that their hands achieve no success;
[13]He catches the wise in their own ruses,
and the designs of the crafty are routed.
[14]They meet with darkness in the daytime,
at noonday they grope as though it were night.
[15]But he saves the poor from the sword of their mouth,
from the hand of the mighty.
[16]Thus the needy have hope,
and iniquity closes its mouth.
[17]Happy the one whom God reproves!
The Almighty's discipline do not reject.

continue

intervene with the high god, others think Eliphaz is merely underscoring the vast gap between humans and the spirit world. Job cannot expect assistance; all rests with him alone. Although Eliphaz does not say Job is an impatient fool directly, in typical wisdom style, he implies as much. The fool's fate includes loss of his household and the endangerment of children (5:4). In his most callous and insensitive statement, Eliphaz interprets the tragic death of Job's children as both something avoidable and the result of Job's own malfeasance (5:7).

Pain and loss are clear and understandable for Eliphaz. He says this in a number of striking ways (5:2-7). The fool's impatience slays him; the fool spreads his roots but around him his family collapses; the hungry will eat what they reap, and mischief does not emerge from the ground. In other words, suffering is not built into the created order of the world; instead, humans manufacture it. Accordingly, Job has brought his anguish upon himself. Eliphaz's belief that humans are responsible for what happens in life, his "theology of retribution," also contains hope for Job. If he caused his pain, he can also act to remove it.

Eliphaz truly wants his friend to escape his suffering and live a renewed life (5:8-16). His advice rests on his assumptions about Job's situation. If I were you, "I would appeal to God, / and to God I would state my plea" (5:8). Job did not do so in his cursing laments in chapter three. Parallel statements about God's treatment of the earth and its inhabitants emphasize the urgency of Eliphaz's hopes for his friend (5:10-13). To motivate Job to appeal to God, Eliphaz points to saving characteristics of the divine. God is creator and rain giver, rescuer of the lowly and mournful, and frustrator of the schemes and craftiness of the so-called "wise." It is the poor whom God saves, so "the needy have hope" (5:16). Eliphaz reminds Job of a theological tradition of which Job has long been a part; God is on the side of the broken and the humble.

Eliphaz then moves from the subject of how God behaves to a theological interpretation of

Job's predicament (5:16-27). Using the "happy [is] the one" saying common among wisdom sayings (e.g., Ps 1:1 and Prov 29:18), Eliphaz thinks God's reprimand is a blessing that should not be rejected. He assumes that Job's suffering is a punishment to benefit him. Job will escape his suffering because of God's character. God both wounds and binds up, smites and heals (5:18). Eliphaz applies his thinking directly to Job's life by changing from third person plural speech (they) about the unfortunate in general to the second person singular "you" of direct address. God will deliver "you" from evils, threats, swords, wars, scandals, fear, want, and beasts of the earth (5:18-23).

Extremely appealing blessings cap Eliphaz's advice to Job (5:23-27). He continues to address Job directly to assure him he will be in covenant with the earth and its inhabitants (5:23). Job will be at peace with stones and beasts alike. He will live in security in a household lacking nothing; he will see his offspring and live to old age, like grain in its season (5:26). Eliphaz concludes with a clinching warrant for the advice he has offered Job. "We," presumably, he and his wise friends, have "searched" it out (5:27). From the sages' long study of human experience, they have known that Eliphaz speaks the truth, or so he claims.

18 For he wounds, but he binds up;
he strikes, but his hands give healing.
19 Out of six troubles he will deliver you,
and at the seventh no evil shall touch you.
20 In famine he will deliver you from death,
and in war from the power of the sword;
21 From the scourge of the tongue you shall
be hidden,
and you shall not fear approaching ruin.
22 At ruin and want you shall laugh;
the beasts of the earth, do not fear.
23 With the stones of the field shall your
covenant be,
and the wild beasts shall be at peace with
you.
24 And you shall know that your tent is secure;
taking stock of your household, you shall
miss nothing.
25 You shall know that your descendants are
many,
and your offspring like the grass of the
earth.
26 You shall approach the grave in full vigor,
as a shock of grain comes in at its season.
27 See, this we have searched out; so it is!
This we have heard, and you should know.

continue

The **arguments of the three friends** are carefully structured. The first cycle is described here; the other two cycles are similar.

	Eliphaz (4:1–5:27)	**Bildad** (8:1-22)	**Zophar** (11:1-20)
Why Job suffers	He is a sinner (4:7-9; 5:6-7) and mortal (4:17-21)	God is just; perhaps he and his children sinned (8:2-4)	He is guilty and God is just (11:5-12)
What Job should do	Appeal to God (5:8) and accept his chastising (5:17-18)	Turn to God who will restore him (8:5-7)	Appeal to God; get rid of sin (11:13-15)
Authority for his argument	Dream; vision of the night (4:12-16)	Witness of former generations (8:8-10)	Secrets of wisdom (11:6)

CHAPTER 6

Job's First Reply

1 Then Job answered and said:

2 Ah, could my anguish but be measured
 and my calamity laid with it in the scales,
3 They would now outweigh the sands of the
 sea!
 Because of this I speak without restraint.
4 For the arrows of the Almighty are in me,
 and my spirit drinks in their poison;
 the terrors of God are arrayed against me.
5 Does the wild donkey bray when it has grass?
 Does the ox low over its fodder?
6 Can anything insipid be eaten without salt?
 Is there flavor in the white of an egg?
7 I refuse to touch them;
 they are like loathsome food to me.
8 Oh, that I might have my request,
 and that God would grant what I long for:
9 Even that God would decide to crush me,
 that he would put forth his hand and cut
 me off!
10 Then I should still have consolation
 and could exult through unremitting pain,
 because I have not transgressed the
 commands of the Holy One.

continue

6:1–7:21 Job's reply to Eliphaz

Set next to Eliphaz's tranquil vision of Job's future, Job's response appears all the more bitter. His experience no longer complies with Eliphaz's optimistic picture of the life of the faithful. Whereas Eliphaz believes Job must be responsible for his suffering, so he can also anticipate a beautiful future once he appeals to God, Job believes God has viciously turned against him. Nor does Job believe Eliphaz has heard or understood him. His suffering is so enormous that it cannot be measured, for it is heavier than "the sands of the sea" (6:2-3).

Job's complaint about the enormity of his misery indicates the depth of the chaos in which he now lives (6:2-7). His immeasurable pain leads him to speak freely. Without restraint, he interprets his suffering as the consequence of God's attack on him. Like a vicious hunter, God shoots poison-tipped arrows into him (6:4). God is a terrorist who both attacks and poisons him. Like his friends, Job also uses proverb-like sayings from the animal world to give authority to his speech. Neither the wild donkey nor the ox make noise without reason, and so Job, too, has reasons for his emotional lament.

Verses six and seven are obscure even in the Hebrew, but they focus on food as a metaphor for life. Job's food is tasteless and loathsome to him.

After his sharp outburst in the previous verses, it is as if he were so alienated from God, he cannot even pray (6:8-10). Job does not address God but speaks indirectly in a wishful manner about the deity. He wants God to respond to a startling request—that God would crush him and cut him off. His death would be a comfort because he is innocent. He insists he has been obedient to divine commands and, therefore, did not create his own suffering, as Eliphaz maintains. The rhetorical questions of the next three verses reinforce Job's despair and desire to endure no longer (6:11-14). He ponders his own strength, his limits, and his support group, and all fall short.

Job repeatedly insists that he has not sinned (6:10) and continually proclaims his own righteousness (10:6-7; 29:14; 31:6). Yet there are moments when he seems to admit the **possibility of having sinned** (13:26; 14:17). Ultimately, Job's dilemma is that only God is truly capable of determining guilt or innocence. As Job himself admits, he may *believe* in his own innocence, but he cannot really *know*, that is, be certain of it (9:21).

Particularly unsatisfactory is the support of his friends (6:14-17). Job's remarks about his friends increase readers' sense of his isolation.

Rather than speaking directly to his friends, he speaks about them in the third person as though they are not present. The ideal friend owes kindness to one "in despair," even if he has abandoned the "fear of the Almighty" (6:14). "Fear of God" in the Old Testament means a spirit of true religion, of obedience and awe before God. Hence, friends owe loyalty to the wounded. Even if he has broken loyalty with God, they should not. In Job's culture, loyalty among friends is of very high value. Job's friends fail him like a dried up stream in the desert or a raging, icy torrent in winter (6:15-16). Jeremiah makes similar accusations against God who, like a treacherous stream, disappears in times of need (Jer 15:17).

Though the next verses appear to change the imagery from water courses to caravans, they are probably continuing the same search for reliable sources of water (6:18-21). Merchant caravans may leave their routes to find water in desert streams only to be frustrated, as Job is with his friends who offer him no nourishment. That only one friend has spoken so far in the book may not be important for Job's conclusion, if he understands Eliphaz to be speaking for all of them. But Job's language of the deceptive waters and the frustrated caravans are not offered indirectly as in Eliphaz's style of speech. Job uses second person address to apply the deception to his friends. "It is thus you have now become for me" (6:21). Then Job interprets the cause of their betrayal. They see and "are afraid." They see Job's terrible suffering that might become their fate, too, if their theology proves wrong. Fear blinds them to his true circumstances.

The subject of their friendship continues to occupy Job's thoughts for the rest of the chapter (6:22-30). He wants to know how he has failed them, or if he has asked too much from them. Humbly he begs them to teach him where he has gone wrong. Once he knows, he will stop speaking. But he does not believe he is wrong for he accuses them of dishonest speech. He mocks their words as lacking proof and having the windy quality of the desperate. He attacks their moral character as callous

11What strength have I that I should endure,
and what is my limit that I should be
patient?
12Have I the strength of stones,
or is my flesh of bronze?
13Have I no helper,
and has my good sense deserted me?
14A friend owes kindness to one in despair,
though he has forsaken the fear of the
Almighty.
15My companions are undependable as a wadi,
as watercourses that run dry in the wadies;
16Though they may be black with ice,
and with snow heaped upon them,
17Yet once they flow, they cease to be;
in the heat, they disappear from their place.
18Caravans wander from their routes;
they go into the wasteland and perish.
19The caravans of Tema search,
the companies of Sheba have hopes;
20They are disappointed, though they were
confident;
they come there and are frustrated.
21It is thus that you have now become for me;
you see a terrifying thing and are afraid.
22Have I said, "Give me something,
make a bribe on my behalf from your
possessions"?
23Or "Deliver me from the hand of the enemy,
redeem me from oppressors"?
24Teach me, and I will be silent;
make me understand how I have erred.
25How painful honest words can be;
yet how unconvincing is your argument!
26Do you consider your words as proof,
but the sayings of a desperate man as wind?
27You would even cast lots for the orphan,
and would barter over your friend!
28Come, now, give me your attention;
surely I will not lie to your face.
29Think it over; let there be no injustice.
Think it over; I still am right.
30Is there insincerity on my tongue,
or cannot my taste discern falsehood?

continue

CHAPTER 7

1Is not life on earth a drudgery,
its days like those of a hireling?
2Like a slave who longs for the shade,
a hireling who waits for wages,
3So I have been assigned months of futility,
and troubled nights have been counted off for me.
4When I lie down I say, "When shall I arise?"
then the night drags on;
I am filled with restlessness until the dawn.
5My flesh is clothed with worms and scabs;
my skin cracks and festers;
6My days are swifter than a weaver's shuttle;
they come to an end without hope.
7Remember that my life is like the wind;
my eye will not see happiness again.
8The eye that now sees me shall no more behold me;
when your eye is on me, I shall be gone.
9As a cloud dissolves and vanishes,
so whoever goes down to Sheol shall not come up.
10They shall not return home again;
their place shall know them no more.
11My own utterance I will not restrain;
I will speak in the anguish of my spirit;
I will complain in the bitterness of my soul.
12Am I the Sea, or the dragon,
that you place a watch over me?
13When I say, "My bed shall comfort me,
my couch shall ease my complaint,"
14Then you frighten me with dreams
and terrify me with visions,
15So that I should prefer strangulation
and death rather than my existence.
16I waste away: I will not live forever;
let me alone, for my days are but a breath.
17What are human beings, that you make much of them,
or pay them any heed?
18You observe them every morning
and try them at every moment!

continue

enough to "cast lots" for an orphan and to sell away a friend. Then he pleads with them for a full and attentive hearing and tries to convince them of his honesty and his innocence (6:30).

Job now reflects on human misery in general and his experience of it in particular (7:1-10). Rhetorical questions embrace the lot of humanity. Is human life not drudgery, the life of a "hireling," a laborer with little or nothing in the way of rights or pay or dignity? Like a slave without protection, Job too lives in misery. The verb translated, "I have been assigned" indicates Job's self-understanding as a victim of some design (7:3). He laments his nights when he talks to himself, is restless, and his skin crawls (cf. 2:7-8). His days, in contrast to his nights, are brief and hopeless (7:6). Despair prevails in his imagination, for he cannot conceive of any future different from the present except for death, an event he expounds with images of life's fleetingness. Eyes will no longer see him, clouds will dissolve like those who go to the underworld, and the dead will not return home.

But it is Job's very despair that empowers him to speak and to express his resistance to God's designs upon him. He has nothing to lose, so he will not even try to be quiet (7:11). He hurls a bold challenge to God. Does God think he is a sea monster or the sea itself, those mythic images of unbridled force and chaos that Job mentioned in 3:8? Job accuses God of watching him and attacking him as if he were one of the sea creatures, and he demands to know why God makes him a target. In Job's view, God assaults him without reason and misunderstands his own being. He cannot escape this treachery in the comfort and oblivion of sleep because God continues to attack him even in his dreams. He would prefer to die and, unlike most religious people, asks only for God to leave him alone (7:16).

To express his plight, Job alludes to Psalm 8 and inverts its meaning. The question of the psalm, "What are human beings that you make so much of them, mortals that you care for them?" (Ps 8:5, NRSV) becomes in Job's mouth not thanksgiving for God's care but a promise of judgment, threat, and menacing presence.

Job's despair continues to drive him. Depending on how one translates verse 20—Job either acknowledges he is a sinner, "If I sin" (NABRE) or in other translations, "Though I sinned"—the consequences are the same. God does not pardon guilt of anyone. But even if Job has sinned, he has done nothing to deserve the calamities that have befallen him. He calls God a "watcher" of humans (7:20), not to speak of divine protection but to accuse God of vigilance in search of human sin. Like a petulant child, he reminds God of his mortality. Time is running out and the two of them are split asunder.

8:1-22 Bildad's first speech

When Job's second friend speaks, it is to jump to God's defense and to call Job a chattering windbag. God's justice cannot be challenged, argues Bildad. After he applauds God's reliable governance of the world, he strikes a piercing blow against his friend. Indirectly but unmistakably, he interprets the death of Job's children as the result of their sin (8:4). Bildad cannot think for a minute that the innocent would perish. Like Eliphaz, Bildad believes there is still hope for Job (8:5-7). If he appeals to God and is "blameless and upright," God will act on his behalf. Readers, of course, know from the prologue that Job is "blameless and upright" (1:1). But for Bildad, Job's moral state has become a matter of doubt. Even so, if Job appeals to God in righteousness, then God will restore him as if nothing ever happened.

Besides turning back to God, Bildad advises Job to appeal to the ancestors and the wise traditions of the past that have sustained many (8:8-19). What they will teach Job is the dismal fate of the wicked, once again implying that Job is among them and must take action to escape their company. Bildad offers a proverb drawn from the natural world to make his point (8:11-13). Papyrus and reeds grow only in water; even so humans live only in God. God-forgetters will perish like the "gossamer" threads of a spider's web (8:14). The godless appear to be filled with life energy, but they cannot grow among the rocks, and they have no safe place.

19How long before you look away from me,
and let me alone till I swallow my spit?
20If I sin, what do I do to you,
O watcher of mortals?
Why have you made me your target?
Why should I be a burden for you?
21Why do you not pardon my offense,
or take away my guilt?
For soon I shall lie down in the dust;
and should you seek me I shall be gone.

CHAPTER 8

Bildad's First Speech

1Bildad the Shuhite answered and said:

2How long will you utter such things?
The words from your mouth are a mighty wind!
3Does God pervert judgment,
does the Almighty pervert justice?
4If your children have sinned against him
and he has left them in the grip of their guilt,
5Still, if you yourself have recourse to God
and make supplication to the Almighty,
6Should you be blameless and upright,
surely now he will rouse himself for you
and restore your rightful home.
7Though your beginning was small,
your future will flourish indeed.
8Inquire of the former generations,
pay attention to the experience of their ancestors—
9As we are but of yesterday and have no knowledge,
because our days on earth are but a shadow—
10Will they not teach you and tell you
and utter their words of understanding?
11Can the papyrus grow up without mire?
Can the reed grass flourish without water?
12While it is yet green and uncut,
it withers quicker than any grass.
13So is the end of everyone who forgets God,

continue

and so shall the hope of the godless perish.
14His confidence is but a gossamer thread,
his trust is a spider's house.
15He shall lean upon his house, but it shall not stand;
he shall cling to it, but it shall not endure.
16He thrives in full sun,
and over his garden his shoots go forth;
17About a heap of stones his roots are entwined;
among the rocks he takes hold.
18Yet if one tears him from his place,
it will disown him: "I have never seen you!"
19There he lies rotting beside the road,
and out of the soil another sprouts.
20Behold, God will not cast away the upright;
neither will he take the hand of the wicked.
21Once more will he fill your mouth with laughter
and your lips with rejoicing.
22Those who hate you shall be clothed with shame,
and the tent of the wicked shall be no more.

CHAPTER 9

Job's Second Reply

1Then Job answered and said:

2I know well that it is so;
but how can anyone be in the right before God?
3Should one wish to contend with him,
he could not answer him once in a thousand times.
4God is wise in heart and mighty in strength;
who has withstood him and remained whole?
5He removes the mountains before they know it;
he overturns them in his anger.
6He shakes the earth out of its place,
and the pillars beneath it tremble.
7He commands the sun, and it does not rise;
he seals up the stars.

continue

In these allusions, Bildad places Job among the godless but, confident that God overcomes the suffering of the righteous, he also promises Job a glowing future. Job will again know overflowing laughter and his lips will rejoice even as his enemies meet their demise (8:21-22).

9:1–10:22 Job's reply to Bildad

In anguish, Job affirms what Bildad had just said, "I know well that it is so" (9:2). Certain that no human can stand before God in complete innocence, he knows the human condition is sinful and broken. Once he had been a proponent of his friend's theology, but now his experience challenges his old theology. Yet no new understanding of suffering and God's relationship has emerged to ease his way. He is in a liminal position outside of solid explanations.

By contrast to human creatureliness, God's awesomeness intimidates Job (9:3-13). The Hebrew word translated "to contend with" has legal implications (9:3). If Job wanted to take God to court, he would be unable to speak because God's power and distance from humans contribute to Job's feelings of helplessness. Job extols God's strength in a hymn containing a series of parallel verbs about divine deeds (9:4-11). But unlike other creation hymns that sing of the harmonious beauty of God's creative work (Gen 1; Ps 104), in Job's hymn, God's deeds are terrifying. God removes and overturns mountains, shakes the earth out of its place, seals off sun and stars.

This God is dangerous, beyond comprehension, and invisible even when present (9:11-21). Divine presence is not a blessing for Job. God might seize him and who would be strong enough to resist? Even the helpers of the powerful, mythic sea monster, here called "Rahab" (9:13; cf. 3:8) cannot resist the relentless power of God. If God overpowers them, all the more, God's presence silences Job (9:14). Even if Job were to get God to come to court, Job's fear would force him to say the opposite of what he intended. God would not hear him out and would surely overcome him with a storm (some translations read "tempest"), a great whirlwind (see 38:1). Even if Job is in the right, he has no hope in a courtroom. He declares he is innocent, but he cannot experience the legal results of innocence, so he despairs (9:21).

Job's suffering leads him to reflect more broadly on the inadequacies of divine justice in the world (9:22-24). God treats the good and the bad equally, destroying both at whim. God gives the earth into the power of the wicked and even blinds judges to the plight of the innocent. If the powerful God is not the one who overturns justice in the world, then who is it? Job asks. He turns again to the fragility of his life, speaking in the first person to describe his pains and loss, but he knows God will not recognize his innocence (9:25-31). There is nothing he can do to establish it. Using second person speech, he accuses God of altering the facts, for God has plunged him into the ditch (9:31). Physical cleaning would symbolize his innocence. In Job's imagination that cannot be accomplished.

Job's observation that God treats **"the innocent and the wicked"** both the same (9:22) resembles a similar statement of Jesus in the Sermon on the Mount (Matt 5:45). But there is a significant difference between the two texts. Job asserts that God *destroys* the wicked and the innocent indiscriminately, thus implying a radical flaw in divine justice. Jesus, however, insists that God gives *blessings* to both "the just and the unjust," and uses this image of a loving God as a model of perfection for his followers to emulate.

A court of law is one place wherein he might declare his innocence, but God is not human, and the gap between them is so enormous, only an arbiter or mediator could help Job. He imagines someone who could control God and protect him from God's might. Such a mediator could make a meeting between them possible and Job might then speak without fear. But this hope is contrary to fact, for no one can tell God what to do. Job sinks back into despair and hates his life (10:1a).

8 He alone stretches out the heavens
and treads upon the back of the sea.
9 He made the Bear and Orion,
the Pleiades and the constellations of the south;
10 He does things great and unsearchable,
things marvelous and innumerable.
11 Should he come near me, I do not see him;
should he pass by, I am not aware of him;
12 Should he seize me forcibly, who can resist?
Who can say to him, "What are you doing?"
13 He is God and he does not relent;
the helpers of Rahab bow beneath him.
14 How then could I give him any answer,
or choose out arguments against him!
15 Even though I were right, I could not answer,
but should rather beg for what was due me.
16 If I appealed to him and he answered me,
I could not believe that he would listen to me;
17 With a storm he might overwhelm me,
and multiply my wounds for nothing;
18 He would not allow me to draw breath,
but might fill me with bitter griefs.
19 If it be a question of strength, he is mighty;
or of judgment, who will call him to account?
20 Though I were right, my own mouth might condemn me;
were I innocent, it might put me in the wrong.
21 I am innocent, but I cannot know it;
I despise my life.
22 It is all one! therefore I say:
Both the innocent and the wicked he destroys.
23 When the scourge slays suddenly,
he scoffs at the despair of the innocent.
24 The earth is given into the hands of the wicked;
he covers the faces of its judges.
If it is not he, who then is it?

continue

[25]My days are swifter than a runner,
they flee away; they see no happiness;
[26]They shoot by like skiffs of reed,
like an eagle swooping upon its prey.
[27]If I say: I will forget my complaining,
I will lay aside my sadness and be of good cheer,
[28]Then I am in dread of all my pains;
I know that you will not hold me innocent.
[29]It is I who will be accounted guilty;
why then should I strive in vain?
[30]If I should wash myself with soap
and cleanse my hands with lye,
[31]Yet you would plunge me in the ditch,
so that my garments would abhor me.
[32]For he is not a man like myself, that I should answer him,
that we should come together in judgment.
[33]Would that there were an arbiter between us,
who could lay his hand upon us both
[34]and withdraw his rod from me,
So that his terrors did not frighten me;
[35]that I might speak without being afraid of him.
Since this is not the case with me,
[10:1]I loathe my life.

CHAPTER 10

I will give myself up to complaint;
I will speak from the bitterness of my soul.
[2]I will say to God: Do not put me in the wrong!
Let me know why you oppose me.
[3]Is it a pleasure for you to oppress,
to spurn the work of your hands,
and shine on the plan of the wicked?
[4]Have you eyes of flesh?
Do you see as mortals see?
[5]Are your days like the days of a mortal,
and are your years like a human lifetime,
[6]That you seek for guilt in me
and search after my sins,

continue

Rather than being cowed by his fearful despair, Job speaks for another chapter and grows more courageous. He announces his determination to speak the truth before God, imagining what he will say and demanding justice (10:1b-2). Boldly, he demands an accounting of God's treatment of him (10:3-7). His questions challenge God's very identity as a divine being. He accuses God of acting no differently than a human oppressor who delights in the pain of others. He reminds God of their deep relationship, for Job is the work of God's hands (10:3). God knows Job is innocent yet searches for sin and guilt in him regardless of the true state of Job's heart.

Job switches rhetorical tactics from blaming interrogation to gracious appeal, returning to the intimate relationship God has had with him from the time of his conception (10:8-13). Unlike his curse of his conception and birth in chapter 3, this appeal emphasizes God's tender care in fashioning his being, knitting him together in his mother's womb (see Ps 139:13). God has forgotten this past relationship between them (10:13). The rest of the speech resumes Job's bitter attack on God (10:14-22). There is no hope for a just hearing for God watches, will not forgive, attacks, and hunts Job like a lion no matter whether he is guilty or innocent. Now Job resumes thinking about his birth as a tragedy God should have averted by not letting him be born. Now Job wants God to leave him alone as he faces death.

Job's charge that **God is testing him** by forcing him to undergo trials (10:6; 23:10) reflects a common notion found elsewhere in the Old Testament. The image of God as a refiner who tests individuals—like precious metals—by trying them in what Isaiah called "the furnace of affliction" can be found in wisdom literature and the prophets (e.g., Ps 66:10; Prov 17:3; Isa 48:10; Mal 3:3).

7Even though you know that I am not wicked,
and that none can deliver me out of your hand?
8Your hands have formed me and fashioned me;
will you then turn and destroy me?
9Oh, remember that you fashioned me from clay!
Will you then bring me down to dust again?
10Did you not pour me out like milk,
and thicken me like cheese?
11With skin and flesh you clothed me,
with bones and sinews knit me together.
12Life and love you granted me,
and your providence has preserved my spirit.
13Yet these things you have hidden in your heart;
I know they are your purpose:
14If I should sin, you would keep a watch on me,
and from my guilt you would not absolve me.
15If I should be wicked, alas for me!
even if righteous, I dare not hold up my head,
sated with shame, drenched in affliction!
16Should it lift up, you hunt me like a lion:
repeatedly you show your wondrous power against me,
17You renew your attack upon me
and multiply your harassment of me;
in waves your troops come against me.
18Why then did you bring me forth from the womb?
I should have died and no eye have seen me.
19I should be as though I had never lived;
I should have been taken from the womb to the grave.
20Are not my days few? Stop!
Let me alone, that I may recover a little
21Before I go whence I shall not return,
to the land of darkness and of gloom,
22The dark, disordered land
where darkness is the only light.

Job's Despair (6:2), William Blake

EXPLORING LESSON TWO

1. What is the "theology of retribution"? What is satisfying or logical about this theology? What is problematic about it?

2. What assumption is Eliphaz making about Job as he elaborates on his theology of retribution (4:1–5:26)? Why does he consider his approach to be hopeful for Job?

3. In times of suffering, we may sometimes wonder if God is punishing us. What does Job's situation and Eliphaz's speech say to you about that?

4. Job knows he is innocent and that the theology of retribution is not applicable to his situation, but this leaves him with no logical answer for his suffering (6:1–7:21). His language indicates that he feels attacked by God (6:4). What is your response to such strong language used against God by Job?

5. What is Bildad's main argument (8:1-22)? What is the danger in thinking about God and God's justice in this simplistic way?

6. We may sometimes blame people for their own suffering, even when we don't know all the circumstances. How can the speeches of Eliphaz and Bildad help us be more cautious?

7. Job acknowledges God's greatness, but in a more nuanced way than Bildad. Job finds God's greatness and justice terrifying rather than comforting because he does not understand it (9:1-35). Can you relate to this sentiment? Why or why not?

8. What does Job's suffering lead him to conclude about God's justice in the world (9:22-24)? (See also Eccl 7:15; 8:14; Matt 5:44-45.)

9. a) Even as Job attacks God for his suffering, he recalls that God created him, referring to himself as the "work of [God's] hands" (10:1-22). As you witness both Job's despair and his intimate relationship with God, how do you understand God's silence?

   b) Have you ever experienced such silence in response to your own heartfelt prayers? How did you interpret or understand that divine silence?

10. Read Jesus' teaching about prayer in Luke 11:5-10. How is Job a model for prayer?

CLOSING PRAYER

He does things great and unsearchable,
things marvelous and innumerable.
(Job 5:9)

Father, our finite minds can never grasp your infinite purpose. Grant us the gift of faith, so we may always trust, though we may not understand, that you express your love for us in every moment of our lives. May we sense your presence in bad times as well as in good. We pray today for those who may not sense your presence in the midst of their suffering, especially. . .

LESSON THREE

Job 11–19

Begin your personal study and group discussion with a simple and sincere prayer such as:

Lord, grant that we may see your hand in every trial and triumph of our lives, knowing you are never absent from your people. May we remain steadfast in the belief that whatever our circumstances, you will never abandon us, for you are our rock and our salvation.

Read the Bible text of Job 11–19, found in the outside columns of pages 46–58, highlighting what stands out to you.

Read the accompanying commentary to add to your understanding.

Respond to the questions on pages 59–61, Exploring Lesson Three.

The Closing Prayer on page 62 is for your personal use and may be used at the end of group discussion.

CHAPTER 11

Zophar's First Speech

1And Zophar the Naamathite answered and
said:

2Should not many words be answered,
or must the garrulous man necessarily be right?
3Shall your babblings keep others silent,
and shall you deride and no one give rebuke?
4Shall you say: "My teaching is pure,
and I am clean in your sight"?
5But oh, that God would speak,
and open his lips against you,
6And tell you the secrets of wisdom,
for good sense has two sides;
So you might learn that God
overlooks some of your sinfulness.
7Can you find out the depths of God?
or find out the perfection of the Almighty?
8It is higher than the heavens; what can you do?
It is deeper than Sheol; what can you know?
9It is longer than the earth in measure,
and broader than the sea.
10If he should seize and imprison
or call to judgment, who then could turn him back?
11For he knows the worthless
and sees iniquity; will he then ignore it?
12An empty head will gain understanding,
when a colt of a wild jackass is born human.
13If you set your heart aright
and stretch out your hands toward him,
14If iniquity is in your hand, remove it,
and do not let injustice dwell in your tent,
15Surely then you may lift up your face in innocence;
you may stand firm and unafraid.
16For then you shall forget your misery,

continue

11:1-20 Zophar's first speech

Job's third friend is immensely impatient with him. He thinks Job is full of hot air, babbling words, and arrogant self-righteousness (11:2-3). Job, he contends, has claimed doctrinal and ethical purity for himself. But Zophar is confident that if God were to speak, Job would learn wisdom and pay for his guilt. Zophar bases his authority on traditional theological doctrine, expressed in a hymn praising divine power and knowledge (11:8-12). Humans cannot know the designs of God for they are impenetrable to humans. But then Zophar contradicts himself. He himself knows the mind of God regarding "worthless" people, a point he emphasizes with a proverb-like saying that indirectly attacks Job as an empty, untamable wild jackass (11:12).

Despite his scathing denunciation of Job, Zophar joins Eliphaz and Bildad to advise Job about how to escape from his suffering (11:13-19). The conditions he sets assume Job's guilt. Job must set his heart aright, abandon iniquity, and cast out injustice. Then he will have a future without fear or shame, and his misery will fade from memory like receding waters. The picture is utopian, for Job's life will be brighter than the noonday; he will live in safety and be at rest.

Prayer Starter: Even in Job's bitterest complaints, we can still discern his radical trust in God amid trials. Think of a situation in your life where you are tempted to despair. Pray with Job's spirit: *Hide your face from me; my love will only grow stronger. Turn your back on me; I will go on trusting.* Where does trust like this come from?

12:1–14:22 Job's reply to Zophar

Job counters Zophar's speech with denunciations of his own. Sarcastically, he ridicules his friends' advice as the product of wisdom they alone seem to possess. But immediately Job asserts his equal intelligence and skill in expressing wisdom (12:2-3). From the perspective of relationships of honor and shame typical of ancient Israelite culture, he describes his suffering from yet another angle (12:4-6). His neighbors' mockery disgraces him and amplifies his suffering, for he has lost his place in society. He names robbers and God-provokers among the prosperous in order to contradict his friends' theology. When he claims that humans can learn from living creatures, he turns his friends' wisdom tactics back on them because he draws opposite conclusions (12:7-10).

In another hymn, Job reflects on God's strength (12:13-25). He portrays divine actions in the world, beginning mildly enough (12:13), but the examples of divine power he draws upon are violently fearsome. God breaks down, imprisons, creates drought, releases prisoners, imprisons kings, and disperses rather than gathers water. God overturns expectations concerning leaders, nations, and the patterns of just political relationships in the world. Though Job affirms traditional notions of divine power, he believes God's power is both unconstrained and destructive of human life.

From experience and observation as a sage, Job claims equality with his friends in discerning God's ways (13:1-2). Yet despite his belief

like water that has ebbed away you shall
regard it.
17Then your life shall be brighter than the
noonday;
its gloom shall become like the morning,
18And you shall be secure, because there is
hope;
you shall look round you and lie down in
safety;
19you shall lie down and no one will
disturb you.
Many shall entreat your favor,
20but the wicked, looking on, shall be
consumed with envy.
Escape shall be cut off from them,
their only hope their last breath.

CHAPTER 12

Job's Third Reply

1Then Job answered and said:

2No doubt you are the people
with whom wisdom shall die!
3But I have intelligence as well as you;
I do not fall short of you;
for who does not know such things as
these?
4I have become the sport of my neighbors:
"The one whom God answers when he
calls upon him,
The just, the perfect man," is a
laughingstock;
5The undisturbed esteem my downfall a
disgrace
such as awaits unsteady feet;
6Yet the tents of robbers are prosperous,
and those who provoke God are secure,
whom God has in his power.
7But now ask the beasts to teach you,
the birds of the air to tell you;
8Or speak to the earth to instruct you,
and the fish of the sea to inform you.
9Which of all these does not know
that the hand of God has done this?

continue

10In his hand is the soul of every living thing,
and the life breath of all mortal flesh.
11Does not the ear judge words
as the mouth tastes food?
12So with old age is wisdom,
and with length of days understanding.
13With him are wisdom and might;
his are counsel and understanding.
14If he knocks a thing down, there is no rebuilding;
if he imprisons, there is no release.
15He holds back the waters and there is drought;
he sends them forth and they overwhelm the land.
16With him are strength and prudence;
the misled and the misleaders are his.
17He sends counselors away barefoot,
makes fools of judges.
18He loosens the belt of kings,
ties a waistcloth on their loins.
19He sends priests away barefoot,
leads the powerful astray.
20He silences the trusted adviser,
takes discretion from the elders.
21He pours shame on nobles,
the waistband of the strong he loosens.
22He uncovers deep things from the darkness,
brings the gloom into the light.
23He makes nations great and destroys them,
spreads peoples abroad and abandons them.
24He takes understanding from the leaders of the land,
makes them wander in a pathless desert.
25They grope in the darkness without light;
he makes them wander like drunkards.

CHAPTER 13

1All this my eye has seen;
my ear has heard and perceived it.
2What you know, I also know;
I do not fall short of you.
3But I would speak with the Almighty;
I want to argue with God.
4But you gloss over falsehoods,
you are worthless physicians, every one of you!
5Oh, that you would be altogether silent;
that for you would be wisdom!
6Hear now my argument
and listen to the accusations from my lips.
7Is it for God that you speak falsehood?
Is it for him that you utter deceit?
8Is it for him that you show partiality?
Do you make accusations on behalf of God?
9Will it be well when he shall search you out?
Can you deceive him as you do a mere human being?
10He will openly rebuke you
if in secret you show partiality.
11Surely his majesty will frighten you
and dread of him fall upon you.
12Your reminders are ashy maxims,
your fabrications mounds of clay.
13Be silent! Let me alone that I may speak,
no matter what happens to me.
14I will carry my flesh between my teeth,
and take my life in my hand.
15Slay me though he might, I will wait for him;
I will defend my conduct before him.
16This shall be my salvation:
no impious man can come into his presence.
17Pay close attention to my speech,
give my statement a hearing.
18Behold, I have prepared my case,
I know that I am in the right.
19If anyone can make a case against me,
then I shall be silent and expire.
20Two things only do not use against me,
then from your presence I need not hide:
21Withdraw your hand far from me,
do not let the terror of you frighten me.

continue

that God is unpredictable and dangerous, he declares his desire to argue his case with God. His friends lie and he begs them to show their wisdom by being silent; God will rebuke them when judgment comes (13:4-13). His passion for speaking grows and he refuses to be silenced; he says he will go so far as to "carry my flesh between my teeth" (13:14). Although this expression does not occur elsewhere in the Old Testament, the next verse clarifies its meaning. Job will speak at the risk of his life. He will defend himself before God, even if God kills him. To speak before God would vindicate him, for no "impious" person can come before God (13:16). Job has prepared his case and reasserts his innocence but would be silent if anyone can build a case against him. Job's confidence rests in his belief that he has not committed any actions against God or humans that warrant his present suffering.

Job shifts from addressing his friends to speaking directly to God, a shift marked by a move from plural to singular verbs (13:20-27). Legal dealings inform Job's imagination about his relationship with God and provide a way for him to describe himself as one unjustly accused, imprisoned, and monitored. But the

22Then call me, and I will respond;
 or let me speak first, and answer me.
23What are my faults and my sins?
 My misdeed, my sin make known to me!
24Why do you hide your face
 and consider me your enemy?
25Will you harass a wind-driven leaf
 or pursue a withered straw?
26For you draw up bitter indictments against me,
 and punish in me the faults of my youth.
27You put my feet in the stocks;
 you watch all my paths
 and trace out all my footsteps,
28Though I wear out like a leather bottle,
 like a garment the moth has consumed.

CHAPTER 14

1Man born of woman
 is short-lived and full of trouble,
2Like a flower that springs up and fades,
 swift as a shadow that does not abide.
3Upon such a one will you set your eyes,
 bringing me into judgment before you?

continue

Job Rebuked by His Friends (12:2), William Blake

[4]Can anyone make the unclean clean?
No one can.
[5]Since his days are determined—
you know the number of his months;
you have fixed the limit which he cannot pass—
[6]Look away from him and let him be,
while, like a hireling, he completes his day.
[7]For a tree there is hope;
if it is cut down, it will sprout again,
its tender shoots will not cease.
[8]Even though its root grow old in the earth
and its stump die in the dust,
[9]Yet at the first whiff of water it sprouts
and puts forth branches like a young plant.
[10]But when a man dies, all vigor leaves him;
when a mortal expires, where then is he?
[11]As when the waters of a lake fail,
or a stream shrivels and dries up,
[12]So mortals lie down, never to rise.
Until the heavens are no more, they shall not awake,
nor be roused out of their sleep.
[13]Oh, that you would hide me in Sheol,
shelter me till your wrath is past,
fix a time to remember me!
[14]If a man were to die, and live again,
all the days of my drudgery I would wait
for my relief to come.
[15]You would call, and I would answer you;
you would long for the work of your hands.
[16]Surely then you would count my steps,
and not keep watch for sin in me.
[17]My misdeeds would be sealed up in a pouch,
and you would cover over my guilt.
[18]Mountains fall and crumble,
rocks move from their place,
[19]And water wears away stone,
and floods wash away the soil of the land—
so you destroy the hope of mortals!

continue

courtroom can also become a place in Job's hopes that will reveal his innocence. He demands protection from God in the court. God must stop hurting him by withdrawing the "hand," a term meaning to have "control over," and God must prevent Job from being too terrified. If God does these things, then Job will speak and listen. His questions set out his sense of his own victimhood (13:23-25). He insists on being told where he went wrong and why God, who had been his friend, is now his enemy. He accuses God of placing false legal charges against him, imprisoning him in the stocks for offenses of long ago, and stalking his footsteps.

The fragility of human life and the hopelessness of the human condition continue to occupy Job's attention (14:1-22). Job's speeches are the words of a distraught and broken individual. Their principal logic is the expression of pain in its multiple aspects, the results of which are circular and repetitive while Job retells his sorrows again and again. Humans have but a short life, full of trouble, as ephemeral as a flower or a shadow (14:2). Still addressing God, he wonders why God bothers with such insignificant creatures as humans. And though Job has just asserted his innocence, he wonders if any human lives free of some guilt. All Job wants is for God to leave feeble humanity alone as each one lives out its life of hard labor.

Job 14:4 is a well-known **biblical crux** (a puzzling Scripture passage). Some church fathers saw in "unclean" a reference to original sin (see Ps 51:7). The verse has also been interpreted as referring to the inadequacy of sacrifices in the Mosaic law to cleanse sinners perfectly, since they needed to be repeated. For Christians, the sacrifice of Christ on the cross provided the only way that the "unclean" could be made "clean" absolutely and "once for all" (Heb 9:12).

A tree, although it withers and dies, has the possibility of revival, but when a human dies, nothing is left (14:7-12). Ancient Israel did not believe in the afterlife of the individual, except in the memory of one's children and in the goodness of one's name, so Job wants his present life to be rich and full, or at least free of his misery. He wishes God would hide him in the underworld until divine anger has passed. He imagines a new beginning when God would call him, esteem him, and stop watching for his misdeeds (14:13-17). But not only are these aspirations merely wishes, they are impossible because God actively prevents a better life with the inevitability of falling rocks or flooding waters (14:17-20). Job may be referring to his sacrifices on behalf of his children (1:5), when he mentions honor or shame of children eluding the parent. All that Job has now is bodily pain and a grieving spirit.

SECOND ROUND OF SPEECHES

Job 15:1–21:34

This cycle of speeches pursues the theme of the fate of the wicked. The friends concentrate on the dire punishment of evildoers, while Job ponders the ways evildoers escape all punishment even as the innocent suffer torment.

15:1-35 Eliphaz's second speech

Although Eliphaz was kind and somewhat gentle in his first speech, he begins his second speech angrily blasting Job for his windy words, airy opinions, and arrogant arguments (15:1-6). Job's speech is dangerous; it does away with "fear of God," here translated "piety" (15:4). Job's own words serve as testimony against him.

Eliphaz attacks Job by suggesting that Job thinks he is **Wisdom** herself (15:7-8). The book of Proverbs presents Wisdom as "the beginning of [God's] works," brought forth "before the hills," and beside God at creation as a counselor (Prov 8:22, 25, 30). God questions Job in a similar way later in the book, asking him: "Where were you when I founded the earth?" (38:4).

20You prevail once for all against them and
they pass on;
you dismiss them with changed
appearance.
21If their children are honored, they are not
aware of it;
or if disgraced, they do not know about
them.
22Only for themselves, their pain;
only for themselves, their mourning.

III. Second Cycle of Speeches

CHAPTER 15

Second Speech of Eliphaz

1Then Eliphaz the Temanite answered and said:

2Does a wise man answer with windy
opinions,
or puff himself up with the east wind?
3Does he argue in speech that does not avail,
and in words that are to no profit?
4You in fact do away with piety,
you lessen devotion toward God,
5Because your wickedness instructs
your mouth,
and you choose to speak like the crafty.
6Your own mouth condemns you, not I;
your own lips refute you.
7Were you the first to be born?
Were you brought forth before the hills?
8Do you listen in on God's council
and restrict wisdom to yourself?
9What do you know that we do not know,
or understand that we do not?
10There are gray-haired old men among us,
more advanced in years than your father.
11Are the consolations of God not enough
for you,
and speech that deals gently with you?
12Why does your heart carry you away,
and why do your eyes flash,
13So that you turn your anger against God
and let such words escape your mouth!

continue

[14]How can any mortal be blameless,
anyone born of woman be righteous?
[15]If in his holy ones God places no confidence,
and if the heavens are not without blame in his sight,
[16]How much less so is the abominable and corrupt:
people who drink in iniquity like water!
[17]I will show you, if you listen to me;
what I have seen I will tell—
[18]What the wise relate
and have not contradicted since the days of their ancestors,
[19]To whom alone the land was given,
when no foreigner moved among them:
[20]The wicked is in torment all his days,
and limited years are in store for the ruthless;
[21]The sound of terrors is in his ears;
when all is prosperous, a spoiler comes upon him.
[22]He despairs of escaping the darkness,
and looks ever for the sword;
[23]A wanderer, food for vultures,
he knows destruction is imminent.
[24]A day of darkness fills him with dread;
distress and anguish overpower him,
like a king expecting an attack.
[25]Because he has stretched out his hand against God
and arrogantly challenged the Almighty,
[26]Rushing defiantly against him,
with the stout bosses of his shields.
[27]Although he has covered his face with his crassness,
padded his loins with blubber,
[28]He shall dwell in ruined cities,
in houses that are deserted,
crumbling into rubble.
[29]He shall not be rich, his possessions shall not endure;
his property shall not spread over the land.

continue

In his second speech, Eliphaz challenges Job's wisdom and responds with "wisdom" of his own. Unlike all previous speeches by the friends, this one does not propose a means of escape. After dismissing Job's words, Eliphaz continues to attack Job's wisdom with a series of questions that undermine Job's authority as a sage (15:7-13). If he was not there at creation, "brought forth before the hills," and if he has not stood in the divine council, how can Job know anything his friends do not know? (15:7-9). The divine council is the heavenly court where God presides over heavenly servants and messengers (Job 1–2). Eliphaz thinks God's consolation should be adequate for Job, perhaps found in Eliphaz's first speech, but Job is not experiencing any such comfort at present. Job is being carried away by false ideas and foolishly voicing anger.

Then, sounding like Job (14:4), Eliphaz exclaims that no one born of a woman's body, that is, humans, can be blameless or righteous. The problem for Eliphaz is probably not women's bodies but the human condition itself. If the holy ones and the heavens are unacceptable to God, all the more lowly is someone who drinks "iniquity," meaning Job himself (15:16).

Eliphaz draws from the established and conventional wisdom of the ancestors about the fate of the wicked in his appeal to get Job to listen (15:17-35). The speech is a harsh warning to Job, and though Eliphaz has abandoned his more gentle approach from the first speech, and though his own anger at Job seems to be mounting, he surely presents his warning to alter his friend's behavior. The wicked one is in torment and terror for his whole life. And referring directly to Job's situation, Eliphaz declares that destruction comes when "all is prosperous" (15:21). About the wicked, Eliphaz piles up statements of disdain (15:21). They despair, wander, face destruction, become food for vultures, and dread overtakes them. They bring suffering upon themselves by stretching out their hand against the Almighty (15:25). Their fate is to live among ruinous poverty only to die young. Eliphaz confirms the wisdom of his warnings by using proverbial sayings. To clinch his argument, he indirectly compares Job to plants in an environment that yields only barrenness (15:30-35).

16:1–17:16 Job's second reply to Eliphaz

Job angrily names the conventional, boring, and useless nature of Eliphaz's advice. But he also admits that were their situations reversed, Job might have spoken in the same "windy" way as his false comforters and presented the same interpretation of suffering as they have (16:1-6). This acknowledgement underscores Job's pain. His former explanations of misery once shared with his friends no longer fit his life. His pain will not end no matter what words he uses.

Whereas Job's friends blame him for his suffering, Job interprets the cause of his disaster to be God's attacks on him. The betrayal of his friends amplifies his anguish. Verses 7-8 contain grammatical difficulties in the Hebrew, but their general movement is clear. Job laments his devastation and speaks of a witness who betrays him like a wild beast (16:9-10). By verse 11, however, God emerges as Job's betrayer. Job heaps up charges against God with a series of violent verbs, accusing God of handing him over to the wicked, dislodging him from his peace, dashing him to bits, and setting him up as a target. God does these things like a warrior without mercy (16:11-14).

Grief for his own broken life accompanies his anger as he laments his suffering and expresses grief in traditional forms of weeping and wearing sackcloth (16:15-17). The poetry's continual return to Job's grief and vulnerability keeps readers' empathy for him alive by making him a complicated character whose anger at God cannot be easily dismissed as the words of a madman. The interlacing of Job's grief and anger make him human, but his insistence on his innocence, of which readers are aware, makes him a figure of compassion. He suffers at God's hands even though he is innocent (16:17).

Job looks for an ally in the earth itself, personified here as a witness to his suffering (16:18). By commanding the earth not to cover his blood, he appeals to the story of Cain and

30A flame shall sear his early growth,
and with the wind his blossoms shall disappear.
31Let him not trust in his height, misled,
even though his height be like the palm tree.
32He shall wither before his time,
his branches no longer green.
33He shall be like a vine that sheds its grapes unripened,
like an olive tree casting off its blossom.
34For the breed of the impious shall be sterile,
and fire shall consume the tents of extortioners.
35They conceive malice, bring forth deceit,
give birth to fraud.

CHAPTER 16

Job's Fourth Reply

1Then Job answered and said:

2I have heard this sort of thing many times.
Troublesome comforters, all of you!
3Is there no end to windy words?
What sickness makes you rattle on?
4I also could talk as you do,
were you in my place.
I could declaim over you,
or wag my head at you;
5I could strengthen you with talk,
with mere chatter give relief.
6If I speak, my pain is not relieved;
if I stop speaking, nothing changes.
7But now he has exhausted me;
you have stunned all my companions.
8You have shriveled me up; it is a witness,
my gauntness rises up to testify against me;
9His wrath tears and assails me,
he gnashes his teeth against me;
My enemy looks daggers at me.
10They gape at me with their mouths;
They strike me on the cheek with insults;
they are all enlisted against me.

continue

[11]God has given me over to the impious;
into the hands of the wicked he has cast me.
[12]I was in peace, but he dislodged me,
seized me by the neck, dashed me to pieces.
He has set me up for a target;
[13]his arrows strike me from all directions.
He pierces my sides without mercy,
pours out my gall upon the ground.
[14]He pierces me, thrust upon thrust,
rushes at me like a warrior.
[15]I have sewn sackcloth on my skin,
laid my horn low in the dust.
[16]My face is inflamed with weeping,
darkness covers my eyes,
[17]Although my hands are free from violence,
and my prayer sincere.
[18]O earth, do not cover my blood,
nor let my outcry come to rest!
[19]Even now my witness is in heaven,
my advocate is on high.
[20]My friends it is who wrong me;
before God my eyes shed tears,
[21]That justice may be done for a mortal with God:
as for a man with his neighbor.
[22]For my years are numbered,
and I go the road of no return.

CHAPTER 17

[1]My spirit is broken, my days finished,
my burial at hand.
[2]Surely mockers surround me,
at their provocation, my eyes grow dim.
[3]Put up a pledge for me with you:
who is there to give surety for me?
[4]You darken their minds to knowledge;
therefore you will not exalt them.
[5]For a share of property he informs on friends,
while the eyes of his children grow dim.
[6]I am made a byword of the people;
I am one at whom people spit.

continue

Abel. There God says to Cain, "your brother's blood cries out to me from the ground" (Gen 4:10; cf. Ezek 24:8). In this poetic way of thinking, blood itself calls for justice as Job begs the ground to keep his cry alive. But the implicit witness of the earth is not enough. Job proclaims he also has a witness in heaven who will speak on his behalf against his friends (16:19). Who this witness might be is not certain. Because Job has just been accusing God of causing his pain, it seems unlikely to be God, although in these verses he admits weeping before God and hoping for a just decision in his dispute with his friends. Job's desired witness might be a member of the heavenly council who could argue on his behalf, just as the satan argued against God in the prologue (chs. 1–2). Or the witness may be the imagined arbiter he wished would stand between him and God in the courtroom (9:33). But Job's hope for justice grows dim because death comes quickly toward him (16:22).

His approaching death continues to haunt him and words about it frame the next chapter (17:1 and 13-16). The imminence of death accentuates his despair, because everything will be over before his world is set right; consequently, justice will elude him. The Hebrew of verses 3-6 is not clear. Job appears to be complaining to God about the wrongful critique his friends are making about him and he appeals for help, for someone to offer "surety" on his behalf. He has no one who will guarantee his innocence, but he appeals to God for such a one anyway (17:3). But then Job claims God is the one who darkens his friends' minds.

To be mocked and turned into a "byword" or popular symbol of brokenness in Job's culture means to be cut off from the community (17:5-6). Job's anguish expands and among his friends he finds only fools who name reality by its opposite (17:11-12). They lie about the world and claim darkness is really approaching light (17:12). As Job resumes his reflections on death, he finds companionship only with corruption and worms that attack the body. These join him with the intimacy of family members on his journey to the nether world.

Job's morbid reflections bespeak his hopelessness and isolation in his suffering.

18:1-21 Bildad's second speech

From Bildad's perspective, Job's words appear thoughtless, endless, and harmful. They are self-lacerating and powerless to change either the reality of the earth or the solidity of a rock. Bildad thinks Job has made himself the center of creation, for Bildad does not understand how profound pain can shrink one's world and alter one's perceptions.

The body of Bildad's speech, however, concerns the fate of the wicked (18:5-21). Like Eliphaz (15:20-25), he presents a frightening picture of the life and death of a person who does not know God (18:21). Perhaps he hopes to terrify Job into altering his speech and changing his attitude, but his didactic approach is harsh and further deepens the alienation between Job and his friends. Like Eliphaz, Bildad fails to mention the bright future toward which his previous speech tried to lead his friend.

Imagery of light and darkness creates an envelope around Bildad's depiction of the wicked person (18:5-6 and 18). Bildad asserts that light and harmonious life elude the wicked in their tents. Darkness, here depicted as an encroaching, deathlike force, awaits the evil ones (18:18). The life of the wicked is one of claustrophobic captivity. They are hemmed in and cast down, entrapped and ensnared by nets and a noose. Once captured, the wicked experience more terrifying tortures (18:11-15). Disaster, death's child, and perhaps a reference to disease, stands ready to consume them. Fire destroys the household of the wicked who are like a dried up tree that disappears from memory (see Ps 1:1-3). Because ancient Israelites believed the afterlife of the individual occurred only in the memory of one's children and in the goodness of one's name, the absence of offspring ensures the utter obliteration of the wicked.

All these terrors evoke Job's own condition. He is covered in sores (2:7-8) and his children are dead (17:18-19). No one will remember him and his spirit is dried up. Bildad's vivid accounting of the destiny of the wicked speaks

7My eyes are blind with anguish,
and my whole frame is like a shadow.
8The upright are astonished at this,
the innocent aroused against the wicked.
9The righteous holds to his way,
the one with clean hands increases in
strength.
10But turn now, and come on again;
I do not find a wise man among you!
11My days pass by, my plans are at an end,
the yearning of my heart.
12They would change the night into day;
where there is darkness they talk of
approaching light.
13If my only hope is dwelling in Sheol,
and spreading my couch in darkness,
14If I am to say to the pit, "You are my father,"
and to the worm "my mother," "my sister,"
15Where then is my hope,
my happiness, who can see it?
16Will they descend with me into Sheol?
Shall we go down together into the dust?

CHAPTER 18

Bildad's Second Speech

1Then Bildad the Shuhite answered and said:

2When will you put an end to words?
Reflect, and then we can have discussion.
3Why are we accounted like beasts,
equal to them in your sight?
4You who tear yourself in your anger—
shall the earth be neglected on your account
or the rock be moved out of its place?
5Truly, the light of the wicked is
extinguished;
the flame of his fire casts no light.
6In his tent light is darkness;
the lamp above him goes out.
7His vigorous steps are hemmed in,
his own counsel casts him down.
8A net catches him by the feet,
he wanders into a pitfall.

continue

[9]A trap seizes him by the heel,
a snare lays hold of him.
[10]A noose is hidden for him on the ground,
a netting for him on the path.
[11]On every side terrors frighten him;
they harry him at each step.
[12]His strength is famished,
disaster is ready at his side,
[13]His skin is eaten to the limbs,
the firstborn of Death eats his limbs.
[14]He is plucked from the security of his tent;
and marched off to the king of terrors.
[15]Fire lodges in his tent,
over his abode brimstone is scattered.
[16]Below, his roots dry up,
and above, his branches wither.
[17]His memory perishes from the earth,
and he has no name in the countryside.
[18]He is driven from light into darkness,
and banished from the world.
[19]He has neither offshoot nor offspring
among his people,
no survivor where once he dwelt.
[20]Those who come after shall be appalled at
his fate;
those who went before are seized with
horror.
[21]So is it then with the dwelling of the impious;
such is the place of the one who does not
know God!

CHAPTER 19

Job's Fifth Reply

[1]Then Job answered and said:

[2]How long will you afflict my spirit,
grind me down with words?
[3]These ten times you have humiliated me,
have assailed me without shame!
[4]Even if it were true that I am at fault,
my fault would remain with me;
[5]If truly you exalt yourselves at my expense,
and use my shame as an argument against
me,

continue

of Job indirectly, but no less transparently, as the wicked one whose fate will appall later generations.

19:1-29 Job's second reply to Bildad

Job begins with the now-expected criticism of the previous speaker (19:2-4). Using a phrase common in lament psalms, he asks no one in particular, "How long?" How long will his friends continue to assault him and endlessly revile him "without shame." In the central section of Job's reply, however, he speaks of his suffering life in terms that parallel and expand Bildad's depiction of the fate of the wicked (19:5-22). The two friends see the reality of Job's suffering but draw radically different interpretations from it. In Job's view, he suffers not because he is wicked, but because God is unfair (19:3). He does not address God in this speech as he has in every speech before. Instead, he speaks to his friends (19:1-6, 21-22, 28-29) and complains to them about God's treatment of him in their triangulated relationship (19:6-12).

Job's complaint shows him to be an angry, grieving person who cannot find enough ways to describe his experiences of claustrophobia and hopelessness. If his friends continue to reproach him, they should know it is God who "has dealt unfairly" with him and trapped him with a net (19:6). In Job's interpretation of his suffering, God is the active agent who initiates all his mistreatment and, like his friends, gives no hearing to Job's cries of "violence" (some translations read "injustice"). In a depiction of his life that echoes Bildad's speech, Job piles up accusations against God who bars his way, puts darkness across his path, strips him of glory, treats him like an enemy, and sends disciplined, unified troops against him (19:7-12). To Job, God resembles a military commander who sends unnamed forces to attack him.

Job then shifts the focus of his lament from God to companions who have betrayed and abandoned him (19:13-22). He lists friends, servants, wife, and other members of his extended household—all his "intimate friends hold [him] in horror" (19:19). He feels the heartbreaking pain of abandonment and isolation, made all the more torturous because it is his closest friends and intimate members of his household who have betrayed him. In a verse difficult to translate, he complains that his own body turns against him as he wastes away and has escaped only "by the skin of my teeth," as some translations put it (19:20; NRSV). Whatever the Hebrew means, it is part of the evidence of God's attack on him and one reason he begs his arrogant friends to pity him (19:21-22).

Job's claim **"I am loathsome to my very children"** (19:17) may strike the reader as strange, given that his children have all perished (1:18). Some scholars suggest that, given the literal meaning of the Hebrew—"the sons of my womb"—the author of Job is using an expression that refers to the children of Job's mother, i.e., Job's brothers.

Though death may be near, Job is not dead yet. Laments in the prayer of ancient Israel often turn from complaint to an act of hope, to wishing for someone who would vindicate the speaker so that the present situation would not be the last word (19:23-29). Job wants his own lament to be chiseled in stone as a permanent record of his innocence, a kind of witness on his behalf. But he also wants a redeemer, translated here as "vindicator," one who will legally establish his innocence. He wants to be declared blameless in his "flesh," that is, in his own body with his "own eyes" before his death. In these dramatic verses Job affirms that his "vindicator lives" (19:25).

The Hebrew title translated "vindicator" is a legal one and refers to the "redeemer" who buys back kinfolk from slavery, pays their debts, and buys back land taken by creditors (cf. Lev 25:23-24, 47-55; Deut 25:5-10). Some interpreters think Job's vindicator personifies his own cry, witnessing on his behalf. Others propose that Job seeks someone who can act

6Know then that it is God who has dealt
unfairly with me,
and compassed me round with his net.
7If I cry out "Violence!" I am not answered.
I shout for help, but there is no justice.
8He has barred my way and I cannot pass;
veiled my path in darkness;
9He has stripped me of my glory,
taken the diadem from my brow.
10He breaks me down on every side, and I am
gone;
he has uprooted my hope like a tree.
11He has kindled his wrath against me;
he counts me one of his enemies.
12His troops advance as one;
they build up their road to attack me,
encamp around my tent.
13My family has withdrawn from me,
my friends are wholly estranged.
14My relatives and companions neglect me,
my guests have forgotten me.
15Even my maidservants consider me a
stranger;
I am a foreigner in their sight.
16I call my servant, but he gives no answer,
though I plead aloud with him.
17My breath is abhorrent to my wife;
I am loathsome to my very children.
18Even young children despise me;
when I appear, they speak against me.
19All my intimate friends hold me in horror;
those whom I loved have turned against me!
20My bones cling to my skin,
and I have escaped by the skin of my teeth.
21Pity me, pity me, you my friends,
for the hand of God has struck me!
22Why do you pursue me like God,
and prey insatiably upon me?
23Oh, would that my words were written
down!
Would that they were inscribed in a
record:
24That with an iron chisel and with lead
they were cut in the rock forever!

continue

[25]As for me, I know that my vindicator lives,
and that he will at last stand forth upon
the dust.
[26]This will happen when my skin has been
stripped off,
and from my flesh I will see God:
[27]I will see for myself,
my own eyes, not another's, will behold him:
my inmost being is consumed with longing.
[28]But you who say, "How shall we persecute
him,
seeing that the root of the matter is found
in him?"
[29]Be afraid of the sword for yourselves,
for your anger is a crime deserving the
sword;
that you may know that there is a
judgment.

as a mediator between himself and God (cf. 9:33; 16:19). Still others think Job expresses faith that the redeemer is God who will judge him to be innocent. However one understands Job's redeemer, the desire to "see God" consumes Job with longing, for only God can declare him in the right (19:26). Though later Christian tradition finds hope for personal resurrection in this verse, ancient Israel did not believe in the afterlife of the individual until the very end of the Old Testament period (see 14:10-22).

Job ends his speech by quoting his friends who find the problem to be him, and he warns them of judgment to come (19:28-29).

EXPLORING LESSON THREE

1. How does Zophar explain Job's suffering (11:1-20)? Although Zophar is trying to defend God, what makes his traditional argument so unconvincing?

2. a) When they first arrived, it seemed that Job's friends were there to accompany and comfort him (2:11-13). But what has developed in Job 3–11?

   b) How does Job respond to this painful development (12:1-2; 13:4-13)?

3. Job's reply to Zophar—directed at times to his friends and at times to God—is fierce and accusatory, but it is also full of observations that many people can relate to (12:1–14:22). What image or sentiment from this fiery speech resonates with you, and why?

4. a) What was the Israelite understanding of the afterlife at the time this book was written? (See also Ps 88:11-13; 115:17; Eccl 3:19-22.)

b) How might the lack of belief in an afterlife of reward/punishment affect the way Job experiences his suffering?

5. The commentary points out that in the next cycle of speeches (15:1–21:34), Job's friends focus on the punishment of evildoers, while Job focuses on how evildoers escape punishment. Why might Job and his friends have slightly different focuses here?

6. Eliphaz's second speech represents a drastic escalation from a gentler approach to Job's suffering (4:1–5:26) to outright anger and accusation (15:1-35). What about Job's words and situation seems to be threatening Eliphaz's worldview the most?

7. How does Eliphaz's escalation reflect our all-too-human tendency to dig in our heels and become combative in the midst of disagreements? How can we work toward a gentler response when our ideas feel threatened or when we strongly disagree with someone?

8. Job admits that he could have said the same kinds of unhelpful things to his friends if he were in their place (16:1-6). Reflect on a time of suffering in your own life. How did this personal experience change the way you respond when others suffer?

9. Job describes not only his physical pain, but the pain of loneliness in his time of suffering (19:13-22). Sometimes we avoid people who are suffering because we don't know what to say or do. How might we remedy this tendency? What did Job need?

10. Job longs for a "vindicator" or "redeemer" (19:23-29). What is a "redeemer," and what are some possibilities for who Job's redeemer may be? Who do you think Job's redeemer is?

CLOSING PRAYER

Prayer

Pity me, pity me, you my friends,
for the hand of God has struck me!
(Job 19:21)

Lord Jesus, you instructed your disciples to love one another as you loved them. In response to this divine command, help us to treat everyone we encounter with empathy, compassion, and love, especially . . .

LESSON FOUR

Job 20–28

Begin your personal study and group discussion with a simple and sincere prayer such as:

Prayer

Lord, grant that we may see your hand in every trial and triumph of our lives, knowing you are never absent from your people. May we remain steadfast in the belief that whatever our circumstances, you will never abandon us, for you are our rock and our salvation.

Read the Bible text of Job 20–28, found in the outside columns of pages 64–77, highlighting what stands out to you.

Read the accompanying commentary to add to your understanding.

Respond to the questions on pages 78–80, Exploring Lesson Four.

The Closing Prayer on page 81 is for your personal use and may be used at the end of group discussion.

CHAPTER 20

Zophar's Second Speech

1Then Zophar the Naamathite answered and said:

2So now my thoughts provide an answer for me,
because of the feelings within me.
3A rebuke that puts me to shame I hear,
and from my understanding a spirit gives me a reply.
4Do you not know this: from of old,
since human beings were placed upon the earth,
5The triumph of the wicked is short
and the joy of the impious but for a moment?
6Though his pride mount up to the heavens
and his head reach to the clouds,
7Yet he perishes forever like the dung he uses for fuel,
and onlookers say, "Where is he?"
8Like a dream he takes flight and cannot be found;
he fades away like a vision of the night.
9The eye which saw him does so no more;
nor shall his dwelling again behold him.
10His sons will restore to the poor,
and his hands will yield up his riches.
11Though his bones are full of youthful vigor,
it shall lie with him in the dust.
12Though wickedness is sweet in his mouth,
and he hides it under his tongue,
13Though he retains it and will not let it go
but keeps it still within his mouth,
14Yet in his stomach the food shall turn;
it shall be venom of asps inside him.
15The riches he swallowed he shall vomit up;
God shall make his belly disgorge them.
16The poison of asps he shall drink in;
the viper's fangs shall slay him.

continue

20:1-29 Zophar's second speech

Rebuking speech introduces the words of a new speaker. The purpose of these reproaches is to counter the authority of the previous speaker, in this case, of Job (20:2-3). Zophar claims Job has provoked him and thereby enabled him to understand Job's plight. After these words, readers might expect Zophar's counsel to take a new direction, since this is the only remark by one of Job's friends to indicate someone is actually listening to him. But like Eliphaz and Bildad before him, Zophar devotes his second speech to a dramatic depiction of the fate of the wicked. His words reveal his growing frustration with Job and his deepening belief in Job's guilt. Unlike his previous speech, he offers no advice to his friend on how to escape his predicament (11:14-19). His words merely warn Job that his present course leads to greater calamity.

The torments awaiting the guilty occupy Zophar's imagination. Four times he names God as the one who enacts the torture due to the wicked (20:15, 23, 28, 29). On this point, he seems to agree with Job's view of God, but Zophar thinks God is justified in tormenting people. Job claims he is innocent and God tortures him anyway (19:3-12). By contrast to the brutal power of God, the wicked are ephemeral beings, according to Zophar. They perish like the "dung he uses for fuel" and fade like "a vision of the night," finally to disappear from the human community (20:6-8).

Outward appearances of the wicked are deceptive (20:11-19). They seem to be healthy and vigorous, hiding wickedness under their tongues, that is, under wise and appropriate speech, and they may be rich as well. But wickedness resides inside them like a poison gaining dominion over their bodies. God will intervene to force the disgorgement of riches like food from a poisoned stomach. And even if the wicked enjoy some benefits in life, they experience no joy.

Zophar's accusations identify specific evil deeds among actions of the wicked; they oppress the poor (20:19). The Hebrew, however, specifies that oppression more strongly as the crushing and abandoning of the poor and as the violent taking possession of a house that the wicked did not build. These acts of treachery result from greed; therefore, the wealth of the wicked will provide no respite (20:21-22). Nor can the wealth of the sinner be interpreted as a sign of divine blessing, as many in the ancient world believed. Instead, for Zophar, wealth is as the sign of devious and evil dealings so it will neither endure nor save (20:20-22).

Beyond lack of enjoyment of the good life, the wicked will experience horrific torments whose originating source is the fury of God (20:23-29). The NABRE and other translations supply the word "God" as the subject of verse 23, but the text uses the pronoun "he" and reveals who "he" is only in the last word (20:29). The effect of withholding the identity of the attacker until the poem's end is shock, since the assault upon the wicked is vicious. Though the Hebrew of verse 23 is unclear, it is clear that the attacker will rain down fury upon the guilty, bring weapons of war against them, set them in darkness, and consume them in fire. The cosmos will conspire against the wicked and reveal their guilt. Floods of anger will sweep them away. The last line of Zophar's speech names these disasters as the "portion" and "heritage" of the wicked, reversing traditional understandings of these terms as divine blessings. Zophar presents a bleak future for Job, whom he assumes to be among those he has been describing.

17He shall see no streams of oil,
no torrents of honey or milk.
18He shall give back his gains, never used;
like his profit from trade, never enjoyed.
19Because he has oppressed and neglected the
poor,
and stolen a house he did not build;
20For he has known no quiet in his greed,
in his treasure he cannot save himself.
21None of his survivors will consume it,
therefore his prosperity shall not endure.
22When he has more than enough, distress
shall be his,
every sort of trouble shall come upon him.
23When he has filled his belly,
God shall send against him the fury of his
wrath
and rain down his missiles upon him.
24Should he escape an iron weapon,
a bronze bow shall pierce him through;
25The dart shall come out of his back,
a shining point out of his gall-bladder:
terrors fall upon him.
26Complete darkness is in store for his
treasured ones;
a fire unfanned shall consume him;
any survivor in his tent shall be destroyed.
27The heavens shall reveal his guilt,
and the earth rise up against him.
28The flood shall sweep away his house,
torrents in the day of God's anger.
29This is the portion of the wicked,
the heritage appointed him by God.

continue

CHAPTER 21

Job's Sixth Reply

1Then Job answered and said:

2At least listen to my words,
and let that be the consolation you offer.
3Bear with me while I speak;
and after I have spoken, you can mock!
4Is my complaint toward any human being?
Why should I not be impatient?
5Look at me and be appalled,
put your hands over your mouths.
6When I think of it, I am dismayed,
and shuddering seizes my flesh.
7Why do the wicked keep on living,
grow old, become mighty in power?
8Their progeny is secure in their sight;
their offspring are before their eyes.
9Their homes are safe, without fear,
and the rod of God is not upon them.
10Their bulls breed without fail;
their cows calve and do not miscarry.
11They let their young run free like sheep,
their children skip about.
12They sing along with drum and lyre,
and make merry to the sound of the pipe.
13They live out their days in prosperity,
and tranquilly go down to Sheol.
14Yet they say to God, "Depart from us,
for we have no desire to know your ways!
15What is the Almighty that we should serve him?
And what do we gain by praying to him?"
16Their happiness is not in their own hands.
The designs of the wicked are far from me!
17How often is the lamp of the wicked put out?
How often does destruction come upon them,
the portion God allots in his anger?
18Let them be like straw before the wind,
like chaff the storm carries away!

continue

21:1-34 Job's second reply to Zophar

Job closes this cycle of speeches by responding to his friends' accounts of the fate of the wicked, often alluding to their speeches. He speaks directly to them in this chapter and neither calls upon God nor engages in a long monologue. Job interprets the destinies of the innocent and the wicked quite differently from his friends. He thinks it is shocking that the wicked get away with their crimes, live abundantly, and go to the grave after a life of contentment. He wants to know why.

Job's plea to his friends to **listen to him** and "let that be [their] consolation" (21:2) reminds us that sometimes the greatest act of charity we can offer someone is simply to stop and listen. In the rush of our daily lives, it is easy to ignore pleas such as Job's, but when we listen to those who are suffering, the kindness we extend to them imitates the love of our Heavenly Father, who listens unceasingly to the cries of his children (Ps 18:7; 66:19).

Job begins by demanding what he needs from his friends (21:1-6). He needs them to "listen." His friends should be able to "bear with" him as he describes his life. Were they able to hear him, he could find comfort. If they listened, they would be able to see his deep pain from his point of view, even if they did not agree with him. If they listened, they would accord him personal dignity and honor, and, like him, they too would be horrified.

Job shows in this speech that he has been listening to them. He responds to their understanding of the wicked and the just punishment the friends believe they receive. Job asks a question to show his perspective: "Why do the wicked keep on living, / grow old, become mighty in power?" (21:7). Job does not answer his own question, but instead sets up the opposite case in rhythmic parallel sentences (21:8-16). Their offspring are secure, their homes peaceful, and God's punishment is absent from their lives. Even their cattle thrive, and their children are healthy, safe, and happy. The wicked and their families sing, dance, and make merry; then they die in peace. No harm seems to come to these people. Yet despite the evident harmony of their lives, they have turned from God and deserve none of these blessings. The text quotes them to reveal the depth of their sin. They are adamantly alienated from God, deny the Almighty's power, and refuse to serve (21:14-15).

Job's observations contradict the reigning beliefs of his friends who hold that sin affects one's entire family, especially offspring. Job now asks how often the wicked pay for their sins? (21:17). In his view, they escape suffering and avoid just punishment. He utters curses against them, hoping for God to do justice by punishing the sinner and not deferring it to the children (21:18-21). Like Ecclesiastes, Job maintains that there is no justice because death treats the good and the bad alike (Eccl 3:16-20).

This cycle of speeches concludes with Job's challenge to his friends (21:27-34). He knows they think he is wicked, but the real evildoers go unchallenged. Because his friends are completely wrong about God's distribution of suffering among the wicked and the innocent, they can offer Job no comfort. And, Job adds, they are unreliable because of the duplicity of their speech (21:34).

THIRD ROUND OF SPEECHES

Job 22:1–31:40

The final round of speeches among the friends differs from the previous two in a number of ways and disrupts patterns established there. The speeches of Eliphaz and Bildad are much shorter than their previous discourses, while Zophar has no speech at all. By contrast, Job's last speech in reply to Bildad is the longest in the book (chs. 26–31). Surprisingly, in these chapters Job often appears to take up the positions of his three friends. Interpreters explain these features in a variety of ways. Some interpreters believe the text was disrupted when it

19"God is storing up the man's misery for his
children"?—
let him requite the man himself so that he
knows it!
20Let his own eyes behold his calamity,
and the wrath of the Almighty let him
drink!
21For what interest has he in his family after
him,
when the number of his months is
finished?
22Can anyone teach God knowledge,
seeing that he judges those on high?
23One dies in his full vigor,
wholly at ease and content;
24His figure is full and nourished,
his bones are moist with marrow.
25Another dies with a bitter spirit,
never having tasted happiness.
26Alike they lie down in the dust,
and worms cover them both.
27See, I know your thoughts,
and the arguments you plot against me.
28For you say, "Where is the house of the
great,
and where the dwelling place of the
wicked?"
29Have you not asked the wayfarers
and do you not acknowledge the witness
they give?
30On the day of calamity the evil man is
spared,
on the day that wrath is released.
31Who will charge him to his face about his
conduct,
and for what he has done who will repay
him?
32He is carried to the grave
and at his tomb they keep watch.
33Sweet to him are the clods of the valley.
All humankind will follow after him,
and countless others before him.
34How empty the consolation you offer me!
Your arguments remain a fraud.

continue

IV. Third Cycle of Speeches

CHAPTER 22

Eliphaz's Third Speech

1Then Eliphaz the Temanite answered and said:

2Can a man be profitable to God?
Can a wise man be profitable to him?
3Does it please the Almighty that you are just?
Does he gain if your ways are perfect?
4Is it because of your piety that he reproves you—
that he enters into judgment with you?
5Is not your wickedness great,
your iniquity endless?
6You keep your relatives' goods in pledge unjustly,
leave them stripped naked of their clothing.
7To the thirsty you give no water to drink,
and from the hungry you withhold bread;
8As if the land belonged to the powerful,
and only the privileged could dwell in it!
9You sent widows away empty-handed,
and the resources of orphans are destroyed.
10Therefore snares are round about you,
sudden terror makes you panic,
11Or darkness—you cannot see!
A deluge of waters covers you.
12Does not God, in the heights of the heavens,
behold the top of the stars, high though they are?
13Yet you say, "What does God know?
Can he judge through the thick darkness?
14Clouds hide him so that he cannot see
as he walks around the circuit of the heavens!"

continue

was copied, omitting Zophar's speech and parts of the others. Some think editors added material to Job's speech, namely chapter 28.

In the book's present form, however, alterations in the previous arrangement of speeches probably imply a great deal more than editorial error or addition. If the present arrangement is deliberate rather than chance confusion and disorder, then the shortening of the friends' words and the increase in Job's words provokes reflection on the debate. On the one hand, the friends' words have lost their power. Lacking further creative insight, their speech fades away as if their point of view has come to an impasse. Job's words, on the other hand, grow in length and authority, revealing increasing strength. His character has changed across the book from the one who wanted to die (ch. 3) and for whom words were futile and inadequate (9:20-12), and who knew only terror before God (9:3-15) to become, in his final speech, a forceful, potent spokesperson on his own behalf.

When Job espouses aspects of his friends' arguments, he is probably employing a device known in Babylonian literature where an opponent takes up the opposite position so no point of view completely triumphs over the other. In this way, the book of Job invites readers to take competing interpretations of Job's suffering with equal seriousness and to struggle with his dilemma.

22:1-30 Eliphaz's third speech

Clearly, Eliphaz was not moved by Job's previous appeals to his friends to listen to him. Eliphaz begins with a series of rhetorical questions about human relationship with God (22:2-5). The questions start innocently with humanity in general, but then move to accuse Job of "great" wickedness (22:2-5).

In Eliphaz's understanding, God is unmoved by human self-worth or by their efforts to be just and pious. Self-sufficient and detached from humans, God's judgments are fair and impartial. The questions addressed to Job in second person singular ask him if it is not his own doing that God has brought judgment upon him (22:3b-5).

From these unforgiving but general questions, Eliphaz turns to attack Job directly (22:6-18). First, he accuses Job of injustice (22:6-9). Job, he claims, has wrongly garnered the goods of poor kinfolk, stripped them of clothing, withheld water and nourishment from the hungry, and failed to aid widows and orphans. These sins involve attacks on the poor and those without protection in the society. Such actions grievously violate Torah and covenant relations in Israel. Job's sins against the poor have led to his misery (22:10-11). But Eliphaz fabricates these charges against Job, for readers know that Job is "blameless and upright"; he "feared God and avoided evil" (1:1). Eliphaz must be motivated to this extreme misreading of Job's life because, if Job is innocent, then Eliphaz's own worldview, his understanding of God, and his sense of his place in the world would collapse upon him.

Instead of listening to Job, Eliphaz hurries to defend God. He asks Job if God is not higher than the heavens, to which Job would surely reply "yes." Then, having set Job up, he accuses him of turning from God. He quotes words Job has not spoken, claiming that clouds and darkness blind God's just judgment. But Job accused God of seeing well his innocence and deliberately distorting justice (9:20; 10:7). In Eliphaz's view, Job acts wickedly just like Noah's generation (22:16; cf. Gen 6).

Eliphaz makes one more appeal to his friend to repent and turn back to the Almighty (22:21-30). Assuming Job's guilt, Eliphaz promises goodness and restored relationship between Job and God will follow Job's repentance. The choice is in his hands. If he turns to God and rejects iniquity, then life will be good again, "light shall shine" (22:28). Eliphaz sums up his theology that God delivers the innocent with more proverbial instruction (22:30). Through spiritual practices, Job can save himself.

15Do you indeed keep to the ancient way
trodden by the worthless?
16They were snatched before their time;
their foundations a river swept away.
17They said to God, "Let us alone!"
and, "What can the Almighty do to us?"
18Yet he had filled their houses with good things.
The designs of the wicked are far from me!
19The just look on and are glad,
and the innocent deride them:
20"Truly our enemies are destroyed,
and what was left to them, fire has consumed!"
21Settle with him and have peace.
That way good shall come to you:
22Receive instruction from his mouth,
and place his words in your heart.
23If you return to the Almighty, you will be restored;
if you put iniquity far from your tent,
24And treat raw gold as dust,
the fine gold of Ophir as pebbles in the wadi,
25Then the Almighty himself shall be your gold
and your sparkling silver.
26For then you shall delight in the Almighty,
you shall lift up your face toward God.
27Entreat him and he will hear you,
and your vows you shall fulfill.
28What you decide shall succeed for you,
and upon your ways light shall shine.
29For when they are brought low, you will say, "It is pride!"
But downcast eyes he saves.
30He will deliver whoever is innocent;
you shall be delivered if your hands are clean.

continue

CHAPTER 23

Job's Seventh Reply

1Then Job answered and said:

2Today especially my complaint is bitter,
his hand is heavy upon me in my groanings.
3Would that I knew how to find him,
that I might come to his dwelling!
4I would set out my case before him,
fill my mouth with arguments;
5I would learn the words he would answer me,
understand what he would say to me.
6Would he contend against me with his great power?
No, he himself would heed me!
7There an upright man might argue with him,
and I would once and for all be delivered from my judge.
8But if I go east, he is not there;
or west, I cannot perceive him;
9The north enfolds him, and I cannot catch sight of him;
The south hides him, and I cannot see him.
10Yet he knows my way;
if he tested me, I should come forth like gold.
11My foot has always walked in his steps;
I have kept his way and not turned aside.
12From the commands of his lips I have not departed;
the words of his mouth I have treasured in my heart.
13But once he decides, who can contradict him?
What he desires, that he does.
14For he will carry out what is appointed for me,
and many such things he has in store.
15Therefore I am terrified before him;
when I take thought, I dread him.

continue

23:1–24:25 Job's third reply to Eliphaz

Despite Eliphaz's efforts to change his friend, Job grows stronger in his own interpretation of his predicament. He wants to meet the Almighty in a courtroom (23:3-6). Legal metaphors reappear in his speech (9:13-21; 13:14-27) as he pictures himself at trial. He imagines God hearing and receiving his arguments. God and he would have a reasonable exchange, and though the Hebrew of verse seven is unclear, Job clearly anticipates an outcome of justice, of gaining his rights (23:7).

The Old Testament uses a wide range of positive images to depict God, such as a compassionate father (Ps 68:6), a loving bridegroom (Isa 62:5), and a watchful shepherd (Jer 31:10). The **image of God** found in Job, however, is closer to another tradition that portrays God using images of violence and terror. The theophany in Exodus, for example, is distinguished by physical signs so extreme (fire, thunder, lightning, loud noise, and thick clouds) that all the Israelites "trembled" (19:16). In Isaiah God "goes forth like a warrior" and tramples his enemies underfoot until their blood stains his garments red (42:13; 63:2-6). The terror Job expresses (23:16) stems from his fear of God's destructive anger (9:5-6, 22-23), which he finds even more frightening since he now sees it as unpredictable and arbitrary (12:23).

But his present experience of God's absence dampens confidence in a just legal outcome (23:8). God is nowhere to be found, although Job searches in every direction. He uses the compass points to lament divine absence, hidden from him no matter how hard he searches. In the next verses (23:10-12), he reasserts his belief that God knows he is innocent (cf. 10:7) and reiterates his claim that he has lived in constant fidelity, treasuring God's word in his inmost being (cf. 13:15). The problem in their relationship lies with God (23:13-17). No matter the injustice of divine decisions, God cannot be challenged (23:13-14). When he thinks of God, Job lives in conflict between hope and despair, but despair seems stronger (23:17).

Job reflects on the fate of the wicked, the subject that has dominated speeches in this cycle, but here Job also considers the fate of their victims. He yearns for God to set times, presumably for justice, and for God to make them visible. Instead, the wicked steal property by moving landmarks and steal people's livelihoods. They feed on the orphans, widows, and the poor. The poor, in turn, are forced into the wilderness to lead onerous, dangerous lives, exposed to the elements and enslaved to the wicked. And, observes Job, God does not act on their behalf, even though they are dying in the dust (23:12).

Imagery of light and darkness dramatizes Job's perceptions of the good and the wicked (24:13-20). The wicked rebel against the light, against wisdom and right relationship with God and humans. They commit all kinds of evil in the dark, treating time as the domain of wickedness. They hide from light and roam about in darkness. The powerful seem to have

Job and His Friends, Gustave Dore

16For it is God who has made my heart faint,
the Almighty who has terrified me.
17Yes, would that I had vanished in darkness,
hidden by the thick gloom before me.

CHAPTER 24

1Why are times not set by the Almighty,
and why do his friends not see his days?
2People remove landmarks;
they steal herds and pasture them.
3The donkeys of orphans they drive away;
they take the widow's ox for a pledge.
4They force the needy off the road;
all the poor of the land are driven into
hiding.
5Like wild donkeys in the wilderness,
they go forth to their task of seeking prey;
the steppe provides food for their young;
6They harvest fodder in the field,
and glean in the vineyard of the wicked.
7They pass the night naked, without clothing;
they have no covering against the cold;
8They are drenched with rain from the
mountains,
and for want of shelter they cling to the
rock.
9Orphans are snatched from the breast,
infants of the needy are taken in pledge.
10They go about naked, without clothing,
and famished, they carry the sheaves.
11Between the rows they press out the oil;
they tread the wine presses, yet are thirsty.
12In the city the dying groan,
and the souls of the wounded cry out.
Yet God does not treat it as a disgrace!
13They are rebels against the light:
they do not recognize its ways;
they do not stay in its paths.
14When there is no light the murderer rises,
to kill the poor and needy;
in the night he acts like a thief.
15The eye of the adulterer watches for the
twilight;
he says, "No eye will see me."

continue

He puts a mask over his face;
16in the dark he breaks into houses;
By day they shut themselves in;
they do not know the light.
17Indeed, for all of them morning is deep darkness;
then they recognize the terrors of deep darkness.
18He is swift on the surface of the water:
their portion in the land is accursed,
they do not turn aside by way of the vineyards.
19Drought and heat snatch away the snow waters,
Sheol, those who have sinned.
20May the womb forget him,
may the worm find him sweet,
may he no longer be remembered;
And may wickedness be broken like a tree.
21May his companion be barren, unable to give birth,
may his widow not prosper!
22He sustains the mighty by his strength,
to him who rises without assurance of his life
23he gives safety and support,
and his eyes are on their ways.
24They are exalted for a while, and then are no more;
laid low, like everyone else they are gathered up;
like ears of grain they shrivel.
25If this be not so, who can make me a liar,
and reduce my words to nothing?

CHAPTER 25

Bildad's Third Speech

1Then Bildad the Shuhite answered and said:

2Dominion and dread are his
who brings about harmony in his heavens.
3Is there any numbering of his troops?
Yet on which of them does his light not rise?

continue

God on their side, but ultimately they disappear. Of course, that may be a long time in the future, but Job thinks his words are irrefutable.

25:1-6 Bildad's third speech

Bildad concludes with a hymnic appreciation of divine power (25:1-3) contrasted with the lowly state of humanity (25:4-6). His words present major opinions of the friends and act as a succinct summary of their theological positions on Job's messy life. He views God as the creator who brings about harm and peace in a mythic battle against chaos. He affirms his friends' sense of the world as a static place, evident in the order of the heavens and sure to be enacted on earth. Before such a powerful God, what human can be judged to be righteous? No human, born of woman, can be pure if even the moon and stars are not clear before God (25:4).

Bildad's reference to women and childbirth is probably not a negative comment on womanhood so much as it insists that humans are mere mortals who participate in the cycle of birth and death over and against divine awesomeness. But Bildad's view of humanity is dismal, indeed, for humans are no better than maggots and worms (25:6). His friends share this point of view (4:17-21; 11:11; 15:14-16; 22:2-3). Humans are hopelessly trapped in their situation and cannot expect justice before God. This perspective conflicts with another view consistent among them that Job is at fault for his own transgressions, hidden and not so hidden. He has power to escape his suffering, if he would only turn to God (5:8; 8:5-7; 11:13-14; 22:21-30).

26:1–31:40 Job's final reply

Job's last speech to his friends comprises six chapters, though many interpreters subdivide it because it contains a variety of literary forms and themes. Job begins typically enough, complaining to his friends and questioning God's abusive power (26:1–27:21), but in chapter 28, he changes both his subject and the genre of his discourse. Called a hymn to Wisdom, chapter 28 appears to interrupt Job's tone, because it is tranquil and hopeful. Many interpreters think it was simply inserted here by a later writer and not an original part of Job's speech. In the next three chapters, Job laments his lost past (ch. 29), complains about the bitter present (ch. 30), and utters oaths asserting his innocence. Together these chapters mount Job's self-defense as if he is in a divorce court where one partner is betrayed by the unfaithfulness of the other. He insists that God name the charges against him (ch. 31). The text unifies disparate poetic pieces into one bumpy whole that expresses Job's anger and doubt along with his last grasp at hope. Perhaps Job's defense functions in the book to draw God forth from hiding.

26:1–27:23 Job's reply to his friends

Job begins sarcastically, demanding an explanation of his friends' words to help the "powerless," namely himself. Their counsel is insulting, verbose, and without wisdom. Since wisdom in Israel attends to human experience, they have failed in their role as wise elders and friends because they have disdained his words about his experience.

The pairing of **Abaddon** (meaning "destruction" or "doom") with **Sheol** in Job 26:6 also occurs in Proverbs (15:11; 27:20). The Greek translation of this term ("Apollyon") appears once in the New Testament, where it is used as a name for the "angel of the abyss" who leads the plague of locusts released at the sound of the fifth trumpet (Rev 9:11).

Some interpreters think the next verses (26:5-14) actually belong to Bildad since they pick up creation language Bildad uses (25:5). When Job has spoken of creation before (9:5-13; 10:8-3; 12:13-25), he has portrayed it as chaotic and evidence of God's lack of justice and wisdom. Job seems to offer a more orderly view of "the outlines of [God's] ways" than is characteristic of him (26:14). But if that is so, Job

4How can anyone be in the right against God,
or how can any born of woman be innocent?
5Even the moon is not bright
and the stars are not clean in his eyes.
6How much less a human being, who is but a worm,
a mortal, who is only a maggot?

CHAPTER 26

Job's Reply

1Then Job answered and said:

2What help you give to the powerless,
what strength to the feeble arm!
3How you give counsel to one without wisdom;
how profuse is the advice you offer!
4With whose help have you uttered those words,
whose breath comes forth from you?
5The shades beneath writhe in terror,
the waters, and their inhabitants.
6Naked before him is Sheol,
and Abaddon has no covering.
7He stretches out Zaphon over the void,
and suspends the earth over nothing at all;
8He binds up the waters in his clouds,
yet the cloud is not split by their weight;
9He holds back the appearance of the full moon
by spreading his clouds before it.
10He has marked out a circle on the surface of the deep
as the boundary of light and darkness.
11The pillars of the heavens tremble
and are stunned at his thunderous rebuke;
12By his power he stilled Sea,
by his skill he crushed Rahab;
13By his wind the heavens were made clear,
his hand pierced the fleeing serpent.
14Lo, these are but the outlines of his ways,
and what a whisper of a word we hear of him:

continue

Who can comprehend the thunder of his
power?

CHAPTER 27

Job's Reply

1Job took up his theme again and said:

2As God lives, who takes away my right,
the Almighty, who has made my life bitter,
3So long as I still have life breath in me,
the breath of God in my nostrils,
4My lips shall not speak falsehood,
nor my tongue utter deceit!
5Far be it from me to account you right;
till I die I will not renounce my innocence.
6My justice I maintain and I will not relinquish it;
my heart does not reproach me for any of my days.
7Let my enemy be as the wicked
and my adversary as the unjust!
8For what hope has the impious when he is cut off,
when God requires his life?
9Will God then listen to his cry
when distress comes upon him,
10If he delights in the Almighty
and calls upon God constantly?
11I will teach you what is in God's hand,
and the way of the Almighty I will not conceal.
12Look, you yourselves have all seen it;
why do you spend yourselves in empty words!
13This is the portion of the wicked with God,
the heritage oppressors receive from the Almighty:
14Though his children be many, the sword awaits them.
His descendants shall want for bread.
15His survivors shall be buried in death;
their widows shall not weep.

continue

may be using a tactic of ancient argument that presents the opponents' views in order to keep any one perspective from complete domination in the debate. Yet Job echoes themes and language in this chapter that he used in the hymn in chapter nine (9:4-13).

To whomever the verses should be ascribed, they contain beautiful imagery arising from ancient Near Eastern creation myths. The underworld, known both as Sheol and Abaddon, lies open and exposed before the powerful deity. The earth and the North, mythic realms of the gods, hang in space. The Creator controls the rain and the clouds and marks out light and dark in a circle. The created world and the pillars upon which the world is set tremble as God rebukes them.

Job's account of creation exalts divine power against the sea monster Rahab and the dragon, the mythic figures of chaos (26:12). Angry storms heed God's design. The Creator is powerful and magnificent. Job's words laud that power of combat against sea monsters, hidden from humans, and cause of fear. This stirring hymn is not completely alien to Job's way of speaking.

The introduction to chapter 27, "Job took up his theme again," smoothes out the interrupting boundary between this chapter and the previous chapter. After chiding his friends and promising to teach them God's ways, Job uses the oath, "as God lives," to declare his innocence with solemnity and to stake his innocence in the highest authority (27:1-6). He cannot agree with his friends and promises to maintain his innocence with a clear conscience until death.

The fate of the wicked reappears, and Job turns the criticism against his friends who, with their "empty words," are his implied enemy (27:7-21). This is where he begins to sound like his friends because he agrees that God will punish the wicked while the just will prevail in the long run (26:17). Some interpreters believe these words are the missing final speech of Zophar, yet the text assigns them to Job. These words may again follow the practice of some ancient Near Eastern texts of assigning the opponent's viewpoint to the final speaker. Borrowing imagery from Bildad (8:14), Job claims the houses of the wicked are no more sturdy than "cobwebs" (27:18). Storms will sweep the wicked away. These last lines anticipate the storm in which Job meets God, though different vocabulary appears there and no one is swept away (38:1).

Job 28:1-28 Hymn to wisdom

The problems of this chapter become immediately apparent to any careful reader. Job changes the subject from his suffering and the fate of the wicked in the previous speeches to the search for wisdom. The tone of the passage changes, too, from discontent to tranquility. It ends with a renewal of traditional wisdom embraced by the book's prologue where "the fear of the Lord is wisdom" (28:28; cf. 1:1, 8; 2:3). For these and other reasons a great number of scholars think this passage is a late addition to the book, added by a subsequent reader to make the debate between Job and his friends more orthodox. That may be so, but in its present place in the book, the chapter serves as a theological comment on the book itself, voiced by its principal character Job. It is as if he has temporarily stepped aside from the debate to comment on it.

In places the Hebrew is obscure. Though some literary sense can be made of the chapter in its original state, this interpretation will follow the NABRE arrangement. The Old Testament personifies Wisdom as a woman (Prov 1:20-33; 3:13-18; 4:5-9; 8:1–9:6), and because the noun "wisdom" is a feminine form in Hebrew, references to Wisdom herself may be present here. She is a controversial figure present at creation and witness to God's creative works (Prov 8:22-36). God acquires her, delights in her, and she, in turn, becomes the bridge between God, creation, and human beings. Some think Wisdom is another way to speak of God, but minimally, at least, she is closely connected to God.

Job begins with an impersonal set of observations about the human endeavor of mining for precious minerals (28:1-6). He observes that

16Though he heap up silver like dust
and store away mounds of clothing,
17What he has stored the righteous shall wear,
and the innocent shall divide the silver.
18He builds his house as of cobwebs,
or like a booth put up by a watchman.
19He lies down a rich man, one last time;
he opens his eyes—nothing is there.
20Terrors flood over him like water,
at night the tempest carries him off.
21The east wind seizes him and he is gone;
it sweeps him from his place;
22It hurls itself at him without pity,
as he tries to flee from its power.
23It claps its hands at him,
and whistles at him from its place.

V. The Poem on Wisdom

CHAPTER 28

Where Is Wisdom to be Found?

1There is indeed a mine for silver,
and a place for refining gold.
2Iron is taken from the earth,
and copper smelted out of stone.
3He sets a boundary for the darkness;
the farthest confines he explores.
4He breaks open a shaft far from habitation,
unknown to human feet;
suspended, far from people, they sway.
5The earth, though out of it comes forth
bread,
is in fiery upheaval underneath.
6Its stones are the source of lapis lazuli,
and there is gold in its dust.
7The path no bird of prey knows,
nor has the hawk's eye seen it.
8The proud beasts have not trodden it,
nor has the lion gone that way.
9He sets his hand to the flinty rock,
and overturns the mountains at their
root.
10He splits channels in the rocks;
his eyes behold all that is precious.

continue

[11]He dams up the sources of the streams,
and brings hidden things to light.
[12]As for wisdom—where can she be found?
Where is the place of understanding?
[13]Mortals do not know her path,
nor is she to be found in the land of the living.
[14]The Deep says, "She is not in me";
and the Sea says, "She is not with me."
[15]Solid gold cannot purchase her,
nor can her price be paid with silver.
[16]She cannot be bought with gold of Ophir,
with precious onyx or lapis lazuli,
[17]Gold or crystal cannot equal her,
nor can golden vessels be exchanged for her.
[18]Neither coral nor crystal should be thought of;
the value of wisdom surpasses pearls.
[19]Ethiopian topaz does not equal her,
nor can she be weighed out for pure gold.
[20]As for wisdom, where does she come from?
Where is the place of understanding?
[21]She is hidden from the eyes of every living thing;
even from the birds of the air she is concealed.
[22]Abaddon and Death say,
"Only by rumor have we heard of her."
[23]But God understands the way to her;
it is he who knows her place.
[24]For he beholds the ends of the earth
and sees all that is under the heavens.
[25]When he weighed out the wind,
and measured out the waters;
[26]When he made a rule for the rain
and a path for the thunderbolts,
[27]Then he saw wisdom and appraised her,
established her, and searched her out.
[28]And to mortals he said:
See: the fear of the Lord is wisdom;
and avoiding evil is understanding.

humans are able to draw silver and gold, iron and copper, even lapis lazuli from the earth. The earth itself is a vast mystery, for though it produces bread, great fires burn within (28:5). Amazing as is the human capacity to extract things from the ground, the deeper puzzle resides elsewhere and is the theme of the poem. As for wisdom—where can she be found? Where is the place of understanding?" (28:12, and rephrased slightly, 28:20).

Many arguments found in Job contrast with teachings proclaimed elsewhere in the Bible's **wisdom literature**. For example, Job insists that wisdom is "hidden from the eyes of every living thing" (28:21). A quite different view is taken in the book of Wisdom where wisdom is "readily perceived by those who love her, / and found by those who seek her" (6:12), and where Wisdom herself proactively seeks disciples (6:16).

Yearning for wisdom centers the poem, as if Job imagines that it is located in a physical spot. He knows that for humans nothing is as precious as wisdom; neither gold nor silver can match its importance (28:13-18). As the sages traditionally hold (Prov 3:14-15; 8:10-11, 19; 16:16), even the most treasured jewels pale compared to the value of wisdom. This observation leads back to the question of verses 12 and 20. Wisdom cannot be found. It is hidden from beasts, birds, and even birds of prey, who sail above the earth and excel at finding food. Nature cannot find it. Both the unfathomable abyss and the sea, here given voices, acknowledge they do not have wisdom. Death and Abbadon, the mythic place of the dead, have only heard rumors about it. The cosmos itself is ignorant of the way to wisdom.

The climax of this hymn is that only God knows the way to her and knows her place

(28:23-28). This conclusion surprises because Job has been accusing God of misrule, injustice, and disdain for Job himself, and thus, lack of wisdom. Now in a surprising turn, he identifies the Creator as one who sees the earth, maintains it, splits rocks, fixes boundaries of the waters, and, then, seeing wisdom, becomes one with her. Even more surprising, Job quotes God instructing humans in behavior Job already does: he fears God and avoids evil (28:28; cf. 1:1, 8; 2:3).

Job's hymn comments on the speeches thus far in the book. The debate has not yielded wisdom, though readers know that Job lives a wise life because of his righteous behavior. The chapter also anticipates the speeches in the storm where God appears again as Creator whose wisdom transcends human capacities to grasp. Finally, the poem serves as a tranquil interlude, a space for reconsideration, and an invitation to readers to ask where wisdom resides in this book and in the world.

EXPLORING LESSON FOUR

1. Contrast Zophar's harsh depiction of God's "vicious" response to the wicked (20:23-29) with God's mercy as depicted elsewhere in Scripture. (See Ps 103:7-14; Joel 2:12-13; Jonah 3–4.)

2. Job explicitly asks his friends to "listen" (21:1-6). Why is listening such a crucial step in accompanying people?

3. How does Job's speech to Zophar (21:1-34) challenge the traditionally held theology of retribution?

4. How does the commentary explain why the friends' speeches become shorter while Job's speech becomes longer in the third and final round of speeches (22:1–31:40)?

5. Why does Eliphaz vehemently and falsely claim that Job has treated the poor unjustly (22:6-11)? What is he so determined to prove?

6. Job once again imagines putting God on trial (23:3-6), but God is absent, so this is not possible. Have you ever experienced God's absence? How did you respond?

7. Bildad and his friends have a very negative view of human beings. Bildad even characterizes humans as sinners, worms, and maggots (25:1-6)! How would you reply to this? What might be right, wrong, or missing in Bildad's characterization?

8. Bildad's speech (25:1-6) is the last time the three friends (Eliphaz, Bildad, and Zophar) speak in the book. Try to imagine yourself in their situation. What would you want to be sure to say to Job?

9. a) What is the basic structure of Job's lengthy speech in reply to his friends (26:1–31:40)?

b) According to the commentary, why does Job sometimes seem to agree with his friends' viewpoints in this speech (e.g., 26:5-14; 27:7-21)?

10. a) Who is Wisdom in the Old Testament (28:1-28)? (See Prov 1:20-33; 3:13-18; 4:5-9; 8:1–9:6.)

b) How does this chapter on wisdom (Job 28) function within the book of Job?

CLOSING PRAYER

Prayer

As for wisdom—where can she be found?
Where is the place of understanding?
(Job 28:12)

Heavenly Father, inspire us to grow daily in our love for your word, which is a source of wisdom and light that illuminates the world. Enlighten us to understand its meaning so we can practice what it teaches, especially in our love for you and one another. Today we give you thanks for this gift of your word, and we pray especially for . . .

LESSON FIVE

Job 29–37

Begin your personal study and group discussion with a simple and sincere prayer such as:

Lord, grant that we may see your hand in every trial and triumph of our lives, knowing you are never absent from your people. May we remain steadfast in the belief that whatever our circumstances, you will never abandon us, for you are our rock and our salvation.

Read the Bible text of Job 29–37, found in the outside columns of pages 84–97, highlighting what stands out to you.

Read the accompanying commentary to add to your understanding.

Respond to the questions on pages 98–100, Exploring Lesson Five.

The Closing Prayer on page 101 is for your personal use and may be used at the end of group discussion.

VI. Job's Final Summary of His Cause

CHAPTER 29

1Job took up his theme again and said:

2Oh, that I were as in the months past,
as in the days when God watched over me:
3While he kept his lamp shining above my head,
and by his light I walked through darkness;
4As I was in my flourishing days,
when God sheltered my tent;
5When the Almighty was still with me,
and my children were round about me;
6When my footsteps were bathed in cream,
and the rock flowed with streams of oil.
7Whenever I went out to the gate of the city
and took my seat in the square,
8The young men saw me and withdrew,
and the elders rose up and stood;
9Officials refrained from speaking
and covered their mouths with their hands;
10The voice of the princes was silenced,
and their tongues stuck to the roofs of their mouths.
11The ear that heard blessed me;
the eye that saw acclaimed me.
12For I rescued the poor who cried out for help,
the orphans, and the unassisted;
13The blessing of those in extremity came upon me,
and the heart of the widow I made joyful.
14I wore my righteousness like a garment;
justice was my robe and my turban.
15I was eyes to the blind,
and feet to the lame was I.
16I was a father to the poor;
the complaint of the stranger I pursued,
17And I broke the jaws of the wicked man;
from his teeth I forced the prey.
18I said: "In my own nest I shall grow old;
I shall multiply years like the phoenix.

continue

29:1–31:40 Job's final defense

These three chapters form another subunit within Job's long speech (chs. 27–31). They begin with a new introduction (29:1) and proceed as if the hymn to wisdom had never been spoken. Chapter 29 presents the good old days of Job's relationship with God. As if in a divorce court, he sets out the beauty of their former friendship. In the next chapter, he laments the humiliation and loss that characterizes his present life (ch. 30). In chapter 31, he utters a series of solemn oaths to declare his incontestable innocence in very specific terms. His self-defense concludes his words with poignant wishes that someone would hear his case and the Almighty would answer him.

29:1-25 Nostalgia for the past

Job's description of the past is filled with lyric beauty. Nostalgically, he wishes he were back in the times when God watched over him and shed light upon him even as he walked through darkness. In those days God watched over his tent and Job flourished. Interpreting life in a way that echoes the satan's view (1:9-10), Job claims his familial and material blessings as signs that "the Almighty was still with me" (29:5). He speaks of his "footsteps," that is, all his endeavors, in language of well-being and fertility, "bathed in cream" and sustained by "streams of oil" (29:6).

During that idyllic past, God's blessings extended to Job's social relationships. In a culture of honor and shame, he was a most honored man. When he recalls the way young people and elders, chiefs and princes showed him respect, he is not bragging in an arrogant fashion (29:7-25). Instead, he is remembering evidence of divine blessing upon his life. In contrast to the behavior of his three friends, his community was deferential, gave him proper space, listened to his every word, and waited for him as if they were anticipating the needed rains in spring. Not only was Job personally blessed and honored, he blessed others by his compassionate concern for them. He reassured, comforted, and led them.

Eliphaz had accused him of injustice, of failing to live according to Torah, and of refusing to maintain solidarity with the poor (29:11-17). Job argues to the contrary. He rescued the poor, the widow, and the orphan. He lived honestly and justly and helped the disabled like a father to the needy. He fought evil rather than performed it. Because he lived a righteous life and had so many blessings, he expected his good life to continue into his old age. The beauty and power of Job's past was strong and his inner life was rich, for his glory was "fresh within" him and his bow was renewed in his hand (29:20).

Job credits himself with aiding **widows and orphans**, the most vulnerable members of society (29:12-13). The care and protection of orphans and widows was commanded by God, who personally extended compassion toward them (Exod 22:21; Deut 10:17-18). Prophets often cited oppression or exploitation of widows and orphans as a sign that Israel had abandoned their covenant relationship with God (Isa 1:23; 10:2; Ezek 22:7; Mal 3:5).

19 My root is spread out to the waters;
the dew rests by night on my branches.
20 My glory is fresh within me,
and my bow is renewed in my hand!"
21 For me they listened and waited;
they were silent for my counsel.
22 Once I spoke, they said no more,
but received my pronouncement drop by drop.
23 They waited for me as for the rain;
they drank in my words like the spring rains.
24 When I smiled on them they could not believe it;
they would not let the light of my face be dimmed.
25 I decided their course and sat at their head,
I lived like a king among the troops,
like one who comforts mourners.

CHAPTER 30

1 But now they hold me in derision
who are younger than I,
Whose fathers I should have disdained
to rank with the dogs of my flock.
2 Such strength as they had meant nothing to me;
their vigor had perished.
3 In want and emaciating hunger
they fled to the parched lands:
to the desolate wasteland by night.
4 They plucked saltwort and shrubs;
the roots of the broom plant were their food.
5 They were banished from the community,
with an outcry like that against a thief—
6 To dwell on the slopes of the wadies,
in caves of sand and stone;
7 Among the bushes they brayed;
under the nettles they huddled together.
8 Irresponsible, of no account,
they were driven out of the land.
9 Yet now they sing of me in mockery;
I have become a byword among them.

continue

[10]They abhor me, they stand aloof,
they do not hesitate to spit in my face!
[11]Because he has loosened my bowstring and afflicted me,
they have thrown off restraint in my presence.
[12]On my right the young rabble rise up;
they trip my feet,
they build their approaches for my ruin.
[13]They tear up my path,
they promote my ruin,
no helper is there against them.
[14]As through a wide breach they advance;
amid the uproar they come on in waves;
[15]terrors roll over me.
My dignity is driven off like the wind,
and my well-being vanishes like a cloud.
[16]And now my life ebbs away from me,
days of affliction have taken hold of me.
[17]At night he pierces my bones,
my sinews have no rest.
[18]With great difficulty I change my clothes,
the collar of my tunic fits around my waist.
[19]He has cast me into the mire;
I have become like dust and ashes.
[20]I cry to you, but you do not answer me;
I stand, but you take no notice.
[21]You have turned into my tormentor,
and with your strong hand you attack me.
[22]You raise me up and drive me before the wind;
I am tossed about by the tempest.
[23]Indeed I know that you will return me to death
to the house destined for everyone alive.
[24]Yet should not a hand be held out
to help a wretched person in distress?
[25]Did I not weep for the hardships of others;
was not my soul grieved for the poor?
[26]Yet when I looked for good, evil came;
when I expected light, darkness came.
[27]My inward parts seethe and will not be stilled;

continue

30:1-31 The miserable present

Grief and mourning quickly replace the beauty and joy of Job's past in this lamenting speech. His depiction of the present stands in sharp contrast to the golden past of the previous chapter. Instead of honor, his community now holds him in derision (30:1-15). In this hierarchical society, people who themselves are dishonorable treat Job as lower than they. Young men whose fathers would rank with dogs, who suffer want and hunger and scavenge for food, irresponsible men without names of honor are among his deriders (30:1-8). They mock him and scorn him and lord it over him recklessly (30:11). As they approach him like an army advancing through the breach, terror overtakes him and all seems lost (30:12-15).

Job replaces the plural of the enemies with the singular "he pierces my bones . . . he has cast me into the mire" (30:17-19). God has become his "tormentor" (30:21). The object of Job's complaint switches from his human enemies to the divine enemy who has cast him off. It is the failure of Job's relationship that has destroyed his life and propelled him into his present. The "mire" is a metaphoric description of his suffering that also alludes to Job's place on the ash heap (2:8) and anticipates his response to God in the storm (42:6).

Job then speaks directly to God, continuing the divorce proceedings (30:20-25). Their relationship is utterly broken. When Job cries to God there is only silence and mute staring back. He charges God with abuse as God's strong hand strikes him and casts him off into the tempest (30:21-22). God is sending him to death, "the house destined for everyone alive" (30:23). Yet Job appeals again. Should he not receive a helping hand in this calamity, particularly since he had shown compassion and care for the hardships of others?

From his indirect appeal to God, he returns in grief to his own relentless experiences of gloom and hopelessness, as if he knows help will not come (30:26-31). His suffering is constant and its effects are physical (30:17, 30), spiritual (30:16), and psychological (30:26, 28). His only companions are jackals and ostriches, creatures with whom he shares experiences of human hatred. He mourns the fate of his body and imagines his whole being as a musical instrument of weeping (30:31).

31:1-40 Job's solemn oaths

Perhaps because he has mourned, complained, and expressed his fidelity and innocence, perhaps because he has spoken back to both God and his friends, Job has grown strong and courageous in his sorrows. His expressive words have expanded even as his friends' words have disappeared. Again, Job calls on God to give him a hearing and court and for God to answer his charges (see 13:13-19 and 23:2-7). In this final chapter of his speech, he sets out the case for his innocence in legal terms. He speaks in solemn oaths.

In ancient Israel's legal system an accused person was convicted if two or more witnesses testified to his guilt. If there were no witnesses, the accused took an **oath of innocence**, swearing before God that no crime had been committed. The accused was then freed in the confidence that God would punish him if he had sworn falsely. In chapter 31 Job swears an oath of innocence.

An oath follows the form, "If I have done X, then let Y happen to me" (see Ps 7:4-6). In an oral culture like ancient Israel, words alone guaranteed the reliability of business transactions and legal dealings; hence, their validity was essential to communal life. By uttering oaths, people gave solemnity to their statements, calling curses upon themselves if they were lying. Job uses oaths to force God to declare him guilty or innocent. If Job is guilty, God will execute the curses, but if God keeps silent, then Job will be publicly vindicated. The catalogue of sins Job offers to vindicate himself presents a highly moral picture, for Job declares all his relationships to be honorable and just. To modern readers, Job may appear as a

days of affliction have overtaken me.
28I go about in gloom, without the sun;
I rise in the assembly and cry for help.
29I have become a brother to jackals,
a companion to ostriches.
30My blackened skin falls away from me;
my very frame is scorched by the heat.
31My lyre is tuned to mourning,
and my reed pipe to sounds of weeping.

CHAPTER 31

1I made a covenant with my eyes
not to gaze upon a virgin.
2What portion comes from God above,
what heritage from the Almighty on high?
3Is it not calamity for the unrighteous,
and woe for evildoers?
4Does he not see my ways,
and number all my steps?
5If I have walked in falsehood
and my foot has hastened to deceit,
6Let God weigh me in the scales of justice;
thus will he know my innocence!
7If my steps have turned out of the way,
and my heart has followed my eyes,
or any stain clings to my hands,
8Then may I sow, but another eat,
and may my produce be rooted up!
9If my heart has been enticed toward a woman,
and I have lain in wait at my neighbor's
door;
10Then may my wife grind for another,
and may others kneel over her!
11For that would be heinous,
a crime to be condemned,
12A fire that would consume down to
Abaddon
till it uprooted all my crops.
13Had I refused justice to my manservant
or to my maidservant, when they had a
complaint against me,
14What then should I do when God rises up?
What could I answer when he demands
an account?

continue

[15]Did not he who made me in the belly make him?
Did not the same One fashion us in the womb?
[16]If I have denied anything that the poor desired,
or allowed the eyes of the widow to languish
[17]While I ate my portion alone,
with no share in it for the fatherless,
[18]Though like a father he has reared me from my youth,
guiding me even from my mother's womb—
[19]If I have seen a wanderer without clothing,
or a poor man without covering,
[20]Whose limbs have not blessed me
when warmed with the fleece of my sheep;
[21]If I have raised my hand against the innocent
because I saw that I had supporters at the gate—
[22]Then may my arm fall from the shoulder,
my forearm be broken at the elbow!
[23]For I dread calamity from God,
and his majesty will overpower me.
[24]Had I put my trust in gold
or called fine gold my security;
[25]Or had I rejoiced that my wealth was great,
or that my hand had acquired abundance—
[26]Had I looked upon the light as it shone,
or the moon in the splendor of its progress,
[27]And had my heart been secretly enticed
to blow them a kiss with my hand,
[28]This too would be a crime for condemnation,
for I should have denied God above.
[29]Had I rejoiced at the destruction of my enemy
or exulted when evil came upon him,

continue

privileged male presiding over women and servants as their superior, but Job is righteous in the terms of his own culture.

With sixteen oaths, Job catalogues sins of which he declares himself innocent. The chapter begins with general claims about God's legacy to humans, a legacy that appears to contradict Job's own experience (31:2-6). He asks if calamity befalls the unrighteous. His next question directly charges God with failure to see. He knows if God weighs him in the scales of justice, he will be shown to be innocent.

Job begins his oath with a central virtue of communal life, honesty (31:5-7). He has not lied, deceived, or stained his hands with bribery or thievery, or any kind of offense. If he has, then he will plant like a laborer, but his neighbor will reap the rewards.

The next cluster of oaths concerns Job's life of social justice (31:13-23). He has treated fairly all claims of his servants against him, and he acknowledges the common humanity they share (31:15). He has never denied the poor, the widow, or the orphan, the naked or the hungry, nor has he harmed the innocent in league with other important men at the city gates. If he has, then his own arm will be severed from his body and God will overpower him (31:22).

If he has abused the land (31:38-40), then the land will retaliate by producing weeds instead of food (31:1, 9-12). If he has even been tempted by a woman or stalked her, then may his wife become a sexual slave to others. Because women were second-class citizens in much of the ancient world, assaults on one's wife were a dishonor to their husbands who could not protect them.

The theological side of injustice is idolatry (31:24-28). Job neither worshiped gold nor gloated over his wealth, nor did he deny God by worshiping the sun and moon as did some in ancient Israel (2 Kgs 21:3ff; Deut 4:19; Jer 8:2; Ezek 8:16). He treated his enemies well and extended hospitality toward the stranger, as required not only by custom in the ancient world but also by Hebrew law. Nor was Job self-righteous and hypocritical, never hiding his sins to save his reputation (31:33-34).

Job's oaths make clear that he believes himself innocent of moral transgression in all phases of his life. If he has committed sins to deserve his suffering, he is unaware of it. As readers have known from the beginning, he is a blameless and upright man who fears God and avoids evil (1:1), but no one else among his community knows this. He does not deserve his suffering as his friends maintain, and God has abandoned him.

Job concludes his words with a final wish for someone to hear his case (31:35-37). Perhaps, like his earlier desire to have a mediator bring him and God together in a courtroom (9:33), he wants his adversary to write out an indictment. This would make the charges public and, above all, evident to him. Or perhaps the document would be a writ of exoneration, since Job has declared his innocence. Either way, Job would be so liberated and empowered by this document that he would wear it before the public and present himself like a prince. He concludes with a challenge for the Almighty to answer him (31:37).

Job began his speeches in chapter 3 with a desire for death to come and for his life and its beginnings to be obliterated from creation. He ends his words, having lamented his many sorrows, raged at God, despaired of his friends, and protested with full force the theology of which he had been a former proponent. No longer does that theology stand. The wicked are not punished and the innocent are not protected from the horrors of this world. One does not always and inevitably reap what one has sown.

Job protests this theology and in the process begins to undergo transformation. His rage at God emerges not as blasphemy but as an expression of his fidelity. Throughout his long, dark night he has clung to God, even if in biting critique of God's management of the world. He shouts at God, disparages God, but he never abandons God, even though he believes God has abandoned him.

Readers now expect God to step forward and reply to Job, but, instead, a fourth friend named Elihu comes onto the stage.

30Even though I had not allowed my mouth
to sin
by invoking a curse against his life—
31Had not the men of my tent exclaimed,
"Who has not been filled with his meat!"
32No stranger lodged in the street,
for I opened my door to wayfarers—
33Had I, all too human, hidden my sins
and buried my guilt in my bosom
34Because I feared the great multitude
and the scorn of the clans terrified me—
then I should have remained silent, and
not come out of doors!
35Oh, that I had one to hear my case:
here is my signature: let the Almighty
answer me!
Let my accuser write out his indictment!
36Surely, I should wear it on my shoulder
or put it on me like a diadem;
37Of all my steps I should give him an
account;
like a prince I should present myself
before him.
38If my land has cried out against me
till its furrows wept together;
39If I have eaten its strength without payment
and grieved the hearts of its tenants;
40Then let the thorns grow instead of wheat
and stinkweed instead of barley!

The words of Job are ended.

VII. Elihu's Speeches

CHAPTER 32

1Then the three men ceased to answer Job, because in his own eyes he was in the right. 2But the anger of Elihu, son of Barachel the Buzite, of the clan of Ram, was kindled. He was angry with Job for considering himself rather than God to be in the right. 3He was angry also with the three friends because they had not found a good answer and had not condemned Job. 4But since these men

continue

were older than he, Elihu bided his time before addressing Job. 5When, however, Elihu saw that there was no reply in the mouths of the three men, his wrath was inflamed. 6So Elihu, son of Barachel the Buzite, answered and said:

I am young and you are very old;
therefore I held back and was afraid
to declare to you my knowledge.
7I thought, days should speak,
and many years teach wisdom!
8But there is a spirit in human beings,
the breath of the Almighty, that gives them understanding.
9It is not those of many days who are wise,
nor the aged who understand the right.
10Therefore I say, listen to me;
I also will declare my knowledge!
11Behold, I have waited for your words,
have given ear to your arguments,
as you searched out what to say.
12Yes, I followed you attentively:
And look, none of you has convicted Job,
not one could refute his statements.
13So do not say, "We have met wisdom;
God can vanquish him but no mortal!"
14For had he addressed his words to me,
I would not then have answered him with your words.
15They are dismayed, they make no more reply;
words fail them.
16Must I wait? Now that they speak no more,
and have ceased to make reply,
17I too will speak my part;
I also will declare my knowledge!
18For I am full of words;
the spirit within me compels me.
19My belly is like unopened wine,
like wineskins ready to burst.
20Let me speak and obtain relief;
let me open my lips, and reply.
21I would not be partial to anyone,
nor give flattering titles to any.

continue

ELIHU SPEAKS

Job 32:1–37:24

Elihu appears suddenly in the book of Job. He has not been mentioned before, nor counted among the three friends who comfort Job on the ash heap, and he completely disappears after his speeches. For a number of reasons, including his abrupt appearance, many interpreters think Elihu's speeches are a later addition to the book, perhaps by a writer who wanted to make the book more orthodox. Elihu both repeats some of the claims of the friends and anticipates some of God's speech in the whirlwind, making his words seem unnecessary. But from a literary point of view, Elihu's speech creates a dramatic delay and builds tension before God appears in the storm. Moreover, Elihu asserts that humans cannot discover God, so God's appearance becomes more striking and unexpected.

By introducing Elihu (32:1-5) and repeatedly announcing across the chapters that he is continuing to speak (34:1; 35:1; 36:1), a narrator divides Elihu's speeches into four parts (32:6–33:33; 34:1-37; 35:1-16; 36:1–37:24). These announcements of continuation may indicate the work of an editor who incorporated pre-existing material into the book or, more likely, they may highlight one of Elihu's character flaws. He is long-winded.

32:1-5 Introduction

Though debated among interpreters, the introduction offers clues to what follows. This is the first significant intrusion of a narrator since the prose prologue (chs. 1–2). The narrator introduces Elihu as an angry man (32:2). Next he presents Elihu's family tree, an honor provided for no other character in the book. It is possible that the Hebrew names of Elihu's ancestry mock him by referring to a contemptuous one who is high and mighty. The narrator expands Elihu's motivation for speaking. He is angry because the friends failed either to answer or to condemn Job. He waited to speak only because he was showing respect to his elders. Then for the fourth time, we learn about his wrath; it was "inflamed" (32:5). Elihu's words are passionate, but they are not necessarily judicious.

32:6–33:33 Elihu's first speech

Elihu introduces himself as a youth, and then chides his elders for not speaking words of wisdom. He spends the entire first chapter introducing himself and telling why he must speak. In the process, he confirms the narrator's suggestions about his character. The three friends are not inspired by the Almighty because the spirit, not experience, gives understanding. He commands everyone to listen to him, implying that he alone has received the spirit. He accuses the friends of failing to refute Job (32:12-14). He even admits he is full of words given by the spirit and is ready to burst (32:18-19). That he does not know how to flatter is evident already to readers (32:22).

In the next chapter (33:1-33), Elihu appeals directly to Job and demands that he listen. Offering some comic relief in this otherwise somber book, he continues to announce that he is going to speak, that the spirit of God inspired him to speak, and that Job should prepare to rebut him without fear of him (33:2-7). Finally, he gets to his point in a direct manner. He claims to quote Job in order to argue against him. His quotes, however, convey the sense of Job's words but not his direct speech (33:9-11). Elihu tells Job he

22For I know nothing of flattery;
if I did, my Maker would soon take me away.

CHAPTER 33

1Therefore, O Job, hear my discourse;
listen to all my words.
2Behold, now I open my mouth;
my tongue and voice form words.
3I will state directly what is in my mind,
my lips shall speak knowledge clearly;
4For the spirit of God made me,
the breath of the Almighty keeps me alive.
5If you are able, refute me;
draw up your arguments and take your stand.
6Look, I am like you before God,
I too was pinched from clay.
7Therefore fear of me should not dismay you,
nor should I weigh heavily upon you.
8But you have said in my hearing,
as I listened to the sound of your words:
9"I am clean, without transgression;
I am innocent, there is no guilt in me.

continue

Elihu's argument begins with a long introduction (32:6-22) and continues with assertions similar to those of the three friends (see chart on p. 31).

	Speech 1 (33:1-33)	**Speech 2** (34:1-37)	**Speech 3** (35:1-16)	**Speech 4** (36:1–37:24)
Why Job suffers	To humble him and turn him from evil (16-22)	Blasphemy; setting himself against God (5-9)	Claims greater justice than God (2-3)	God punishes the hard-hearted (36:5-15)
What Job should do	Pray and confess (26-27)	Admit wrongdoing (32-33)	Consider the majesty of God (4-8)	Trust and praise God (36:16-25)
Authority for his argument	Wisdom (33)	Arguments of the wise (34-37)	God hears and is just (13-16)	Greatness of God (36:26–37:24)

10Yet he invents pretexts against me
and counts me as an enemy.
11He puts my feet in the stocks,
watches all my paths!"
12In this you are not just, let me tell you;
for God is greater than mortals.
13Why, then, do you make complaint against him
that he gives no reply to their words?
14For God does speak, once,
even twice, though you do not see it:
15In a dream, in a vision of the night,
when deep sleep falls upon mortals
as they slumber in their beds.
16It is then he opens their ears
and with a warning, terrifies them,
17By turning mortals from acting
and keeping pride away from a man,
18He holds his soul from the pit,
his life from passing to the grave.
19Or he is chastened on a bed of pain,
suffering continually in his bones,
20So that to his appetite food is repulsive,
his throat rejects the choicest nourishment.
21His flesh is wasted, it cannot be seen;
bones, once invisible, appear;
22His soul draws near to the pit,
his life to the place of the dead.
23If then there be a divine messenger,
a mediator, one out of a thousand,
to show him what is right,
24He will take pity on him and say,
"Deliver him from going down to the pit;
I have found him a ransom."
25Then his flesh shall become soft as a boy's;
he shall be again as in the days of his youth.
26He shall pray and God will favor him;
he shall see God's face with rejoicing;
for he restores a person's righteousness.
27He shall sing before all and say,
"I sinned and did wrong,
yet I was not punished accordingly.
28He delivered me from passing to the pit,
and my life sees light."
29See, all these things God does,
two, even three times, for a man,
30Bringing back his soul from the pit
to the light, in the light of the living.
31Be attentive, Job, listen to me!
Be silent and I will speak.
32If you have anything to say, then answer me.
Speak out! I should like to see you justified.
33If not, then you listen to me;
be silent, and I will teach you wisdom.

CHAPTER 34

1Then Elihu answered and said:

2Hear my discourse, you that are wise;
you that have knowledge, listen to me!
3For the ear tests words,
as the palate tastes food.
4Let us choose what is right;
let us determine among ourselves what is good.
5For Job has said, "I am innocent,
but God has taken away what is my right.
6I declare the judgment on me to be a lie;
my arrow-wound is incurable, sinless though I am."
7What man is like Job?
He drinks in blasphemies like water,
8Keeps company with evildoers
and goes along with the wicked,
9When he says, "There is no profit
in pleasing God."
10Therefore, you that have understanding, hear me:
far be it from God to do wickedness;
far from the Almighty to do wrong!
11Rather, he requites mortals for their conduct,
and brings home to them their way of life.
12Surely, God cannot act wickedly,
the Almighty cannot pervert justice.

continue

is unjust to God. Because God is greater than humans, Job has no place in demanding an account. When God does speak, one may not even know it. When God warns with terrors of the night or sends illness and suffering, it is to save the person from death (33:14-22).

Like Job, Elihu also hopes for a mediator between God and humans, not to control God as Job had hoped (9:32-35), or to witness on Job's behalf (16:19), but to bring Job around and save him. Elihu and Job have opposite opinions as to the role of the heavenly mediator. The effects of the mediator's guidance will be to restore Job to singing and rejoicing as God restores his soul from the realm of death (33:25-30). In an arrogant manner, Elihu urges Job to listen silently, unless he has something to say. As a younger man speaking to an elder in a culture that honors the elder, he is quite overbearing. Perhaps he thinks he is Job's mediator.

34:1-37 Elihu's second speech

Elihu treats Job's three friends with the same disrespect he shows Job, addressing them as wise men while he mocks their wisdom. He invites them to discern the truth with him, though he has already decided what it is. Again he quotes Job to discredit his speech, interpreting his words and his person as evil. With even more arrogance, he instructs the friends about God's justice in traditional terms (34:10-15). God does not respect humans for wealth or power but focuses on their ways and dispenses justice with inescapable speed. He condemns Job further by assuming that the wise will agree with him in dismissing Job's claim to wisdom. He deserves punishment because his rebellious words compound his sins.

Elihu's insistence on the **omniscience of God** mirrors a similar sentiment found in Psalm 139. Elihu uses the metaphor of vision, noting that even the densest darkness cannot prevent God from observing our actions (34:21-22). Psalm 139 expands this idea, describing how God sees not only our external actions but also our innermost thoughts (139:2-4). The psalm also alludes to God's omnipresence, assuring us that wherever we go God is always there (139:5-10). Because of this presence, even darkness becomes light (139:11-12).

The Wrath of Elihu (32:6), William Blake

13Who gave him charge over the earth,
or who set all the world in its place?
14If he were to set his mind to it,
gather to himself his spirit and breath,
15All flesh would perish together,
and mortals return to dust.
16Now you—understand, hear this!
Listen to the words I speak!
17Can an enemy of justice be in control,
will you condemn the supreme Just One,
18Who says to a king, "You are worthless!"
and to nobles, "You are wicked!"
19Who neither favors the person of princes,
nor respects the rich more than the poor?
For they are all the work of his hands;
20in a moment they die, even at midnight.
People are shaken, and pass away,
the powerful are removed without lifting
a hand;
21For his eyes are upon our ways,
and all our steps he sees.
22There is no darkness so dense
that evildoers can hide in it.
23For no one has God set a time
to come before him in judgment.
24Without inquiry he shatters the mighty,
and appoints others in their place,
25Thus he discerns their works;
overnight they are crushed.
26Where the wicked are, he strikes them,
in a place where all can see,
27Because they turned away from him
and did not understand his ways at all:
28And made the cry of the poor reach him,
so that he heard the cry of the afflicted.
29If he is silent, who then can condemn?
If he hides his face, who then can behold
him,
whether nation or individual?
30Let an impious man not rule,
nor those who ensnare their people.
31Should anyone say to God,
"I accept my punishment; I will offend no
more;
32What I cannot see, teach me:
if I have done wrong, I will do so no more,"
33Would you then say that God must punish,
when you are disdainful?
It is you who must choose, not I;
speak, therefore, what you know.
34Those who understand will say to me,
all the wise who hear my views:
35"Job speaks without knowledge,
his words make no sense.
36Let Job be tested to the limit,
since his answers are those of the impious;
37For he is adding rebellion to his sin
by brushing off our arguments
and addressing many words to God."

CHAPTER 35

1Then Elihu answered and said:

2Do you think it right to say,
"I am in the right, not God"?
3When you ask what it profits you,
"What advantage do I have from not
sinning?"
4I have words for a reply to you
and your friends as well.
5Look up to the skies and see;
behold the heavens high above you.
6If you sin, what do you do to God?
Even if your offenses are many, how do
you affect him?
7If you are righteous, what do you give him,
or what does he receive from your hand?
8Your wickedness affects only someone like
yourself,
and your justice, only a fellow human
being.
9In great oppression people cry out;
they call for help because of the power of
the great,
10No one says, "Where is God, my Maker,
who gives songs in the night,
11Teaches us more than the beasts of the
earth,

continue

and makes us wiser than the birds of the
heavens?"
12Though thus they cry out, he does not
answer
because of the pride of the wicked.
13But it is idle to say God does not hear
or that the Almighty does not take notice.
14Even though you say, "You take no notice
of it,"
the case is before him; with trembling
wait upon him.
15But now that you have done otherwise,
God's anger punishes,
nor does he show much concern over a
life.
16Yet Job to no purpose opens his mouth,
multiplying words without knowledge.

CHAPTER 36

1Elihu continued and said:

2Wait a little and I will instruct you,
for there are still words to be said for God.
3I will assemble arguments from afar,
and for my maker I will establish what is
right.
4For indeed, my words are not a lie;
one perfect in knowledge is before you.
5Look, God is great, not disdainful;
his strength of purpose is great.
He does not preserve the life of the wicked.
6He establishes the right of the poor;
he does not divert his eyes from the just
7But he seats them upon thrones
with kings, exalted forever.
8If they are bound with fetters,
held fast by bonds of affliction,
9He lets them know what they have done,
and how arrogant are their sins.
10He opens their ears to correction
and tells them to turn back from evil.
11If they listen and serve him,
they spend their days in prosperity,
their years in happiness.
12But if they do not listen, they pass to the
grave,
they perish for lack of knowledge.
13The impious in heart lay up anger;
they do not cry for help when he binds
them;
14They will die young—
their life among the reprobate.
15But he saves the afflicted through their
affliction,
and opens their ears through oppression.
16He entices you from distress,
to a broad place without constraint;
what rests on your table is rich food.
17Though you are full of the judgment of the
wicked,
judgment and justice will be maintained.

continue

35:1-16 Elihu's third speech

Elihu continues interrogating Job. Why does Job think it proper to claim he is just and God is not? (35:1-3). He wants Job to recognize and submit to the transcendence of God beyond all things human (35:4-12). No human behavior can affect God, even that of the oppressed who cry out. God does not respond to human cries. The Hebrew of the next verses is not entirely clear, but Elihu maintains that Job's words are meaningless (35:16).

36:1–37:24 Elihu's fourth speech

Elihu keeps his windbag character by telling us again that he is going to speak to illuminate Job's situation (36:2-4). When he finally gets to the knowledge he brings "from afar" (36:3), it amounts to reiteration of arguments already given by the friends that God rewards the good and punishes the wicked (36:4-21). Though God is not affected by any human behavior according to the previous chapter, God does respond to human behavior by punishing the wicked.

18Let not anger at abundance entice you,
nor great bribery lead you astray.
19Will your wealth equip you against distress,
or all your exertions of strength?
20Do not long for the night,
when peoples vanish in their place.
21Be careful; do not turn to evil;
for this you have preferred to affliction.
22Look, God is exalted in his power.
What teacher is there like him?
23Who prescribes for him his way?
Who says, "You have done wrong"?
24Remember, you should extol his work,
which people have praised in song.
25All humankind beholds it;
everyone views it from afar.
26See, God is great beyond our knowledge,
the number of his years past searching out.
27He holds in check the waterdrops
that filter in rain from his flood,
28Till the clouds flow with them
and they rain down on all humankind.
29Can anyone understand the spreading clouds,
the thunderings from his tent?
30Look, he spreads his light over it,
it covers the roots of the sea.
31For by these he judges the nations,
and gives food in abundance.
32In his hands he holds the lightning,
and he commands it to strike the mark.
33His thunder announces him
and incites the fury of the storm.

CHAPTER 37

1At this my heart trembles
and leaps out of its place.
2Listen to his angry voice
and the rumble that comes forth from his mouth!
3Everywhere under the heavens he sends it,
with his light, to the ends of the earth.
4Again his voice roars,
his majestic voice thunders;
he does not restrain them when his voice is heard.
5God thunders forth marvels with his voice;
he does great things beyond our knowing.
6He says to the snow, "Fall to the earth";
likewise to his heavy, drenching rain.
7He shuts up all humankind indoors,
so that all people may know his work.
8The wild beasts take to cover
and remain quiet in their dens.
9Out of its chamber the tempest comes forth;
from the north winds, the cold.
10With his breath God brings the frost,
and the broad waters congeal.
11The clouds too are laden with moisture,
the storm-cloud scatters its light.
12He it is who changes their rounds,
according to his plans,
to do all that he commands them
across the inhabited world.
13Whether for punishment or mercy,
he makes it happen.
14Listen to this, Job!
Stand and consider the marvels of God!
15Do you know how God lays his command upon them,
and makes the light shine forth from his clouds?
16Do you know how the clouds are banked,
the marvels of him who is perfect in knowledge?
17You, who swelter in your clothes
when calm lies over the land from the south,
18Can you with him spread out the firmament of the skies,
hard as a molten mirror?
19Teach us then what we shall say to him;
we cannot, for the darkness, make our plea.

continue

God reveals sins to correct the disobedient and causes the disobedient to perish. Suffering and distress are educational for some and God sends affliction to save them (36:15). Verses 16-21 are nearly unreadable in the Hebrew.

Much of the remainder of Elihu's speech anticipates the words of God in the storm (36:22–37:22). His theme is the power and wonder of creation. He advises Job to consider that God is transcendent, beyond human connection, as revealed in God's providential control of the cosmos (36:22-25). In the ancient world, the workings of sun and rain, of stars and seasons, were profound mysteries. Elihu finds a nearly sacramental sense in the world, an expression of divine life when God uses the rains to nourish nations and provide food (36:26-32). Offering personal testimony, he speaks of storms as God's angry and controlling voice (36:33–37:9). Even hail and frost serve God's purposes (37:10-13).

Elihu commands Job to listen and contemplate God's works. He demands to know if Job understands how God creates light behind clouds, and if Job participates in creating the firmament with God (37:15-18). After six long chapters, he concludes that humans cannot discover the Almighty because God is beyond all accounting. None can see him (37:22-24).

20Will he be told about it when I speak?
Can anyone talk when he is being
destroyed?
21Rather, it is as the light that cannot be seen
while it is obscured by the clouds,
till the wind comes by and sweeps them
away.
22From Zaphon the golden splendor comes,
surrounding God's awesome majesty!
23The Almighty! We cannot find him,
preeminent in power and judgment,
abundant in justice, who never oppresses.
24Therefore people fear him;
none can see him, however wise their
hearts.

Surely Elihu is an intruder on the scene, but his speech acts as a thematic bridge between the debates of Job and his friends and the speeches of God still to come. In comic, bombastic terms that violate the customs of the day and disrespect the previous speakers, Elihu builds anticipation and makes Job's three older friends look good by comparison.

EXPLORING LESSON FIVE

1. What is the basic structure of Job 29–31, which is a subunit within Job's long speech (Job 27–31)?

2. In remembering the "good old times" of his past, Job recalls that he was not only prosperous and happy but that he was a righteous man who served others. What are some of the ways Job describes his care for the vulnerable (29:12-25)?

3. Job's lament in chapter 30 is especially powerful following his sincere description of his care for others in chapter 29. Do you believe there is a difference between *complaining* and *lamenting*? If so, how would you explain this difference?

4. Look back at Job's original reaction to his misfortune (1:20-22; 2:8-10). Why do you think Job's response has changed so significantly? Can you relate to both types of responses to suffering?

5. What is Job's purpose in using a series of oaths to defend himself (31:5-40)?

6. Job's oaths serve as an examination of conscience as he reviews his life and relationships. What role does an examination of conscience play in your spiritual life?

7. a) Why do some Scripture scholars think Elihu's speeches (32:1–37:24) are a later addition to the book of Job?

   b) What "character flaw" does the commentary assign to Elihu as a result of his four-part speech?

8. What does the narrator of the book of Job tell us about Elihu (32:1-5)? How might this description influence the way we read and interpret his speech?

9. Elihu's instinct to defend God is a natural one, but what complex human experience(s) does his defense of God overlook (34:10-37; 36:4-21)?

10. What truth does Elihu communicate about God in his final speech, which prepares the reader for God's appearance in the chapters to come (36:24–37:24)?

CLOSING PRAYER

Therefore people fear him;
none can see him, however wise their hearts. (Job 37:24)

Eternal God, you remained hidden from our ancestors in faith until, in the fullness of time, you revealed yourself fully through your beloved Son, Jesus Christ. We offer you praise and thanksgiving for the gift of your Word made flesh. Help us to express our gratitude through devoted discipleship in thought and deed, especially . . .

LESSON SIX

Job 38–42

Begin your personal study and group discussion with a simple and sincere prayer such as:

Lord, grant that we may see your hand in every trial and triumph of our lives, knowing you are never absent from your people. May we remain steadfast in the belief that whatever our circumstances, you will never abandon us, for you are our rock and our salvation.

Read the Bible text of Job 38–42, found in the outside columns of pages 104–118, highlighting what stands out to you.

Read the accompanying commentary to add to your understanding.

Respond to the questions on pages 119–121, Exploring Lesson Six.

The Closing Prayer on page 122 is for your personal use and may be used at the end of group discussion.

VIII. The Lord and Job Meet

CHAPTER 38

1 Then the Lord answered Job out of the storm
and said:

2 Who is this who darkens counsel
with words of ignorance?
3 Gird up your loins now, like a man;
I will question you, and you tell me the
answers!
4 Where were you when I founded the earth?
Tell me, if you have understanding.
5 Who determined its size? Surely you know?
Who stretched out the measuring line for
it?
6 Into what were its pedestals sunk,
and who laid its cornerstone,
7 While the morning stars sang together
and all the sons of God shouted for joy?
8 Who shut within doors the sea,
when it burst forth from the womb,
9 When I made the clouds its garment
and thick darkness its swaddling bands?
10 When I set limits for it
and fastened the bar of its door,
11 And said: Thus far shall you come but no
farther,
and here shall your proud waves stop?
12 Have you ever in your lifetime commanded
the morning

continue

THE SPEECHES IN THE STORM

Job 38:1–42:6

Elihu's insistence that "we cannot find" God (37:23) makes God's appearance in the storm all the more dramatic and surprising. Job alone hoped for such a meeting, but the friends insisted God was inaccessible and did not need to speak because divine justice was already clearly revealed in human life and in the world of animals and plants. In these speeches, as in the prologue, God's name again becomes Yahweh, ("the Lord"), the personal name revealed in Exodus 3. Throughout the long debates between Job and his friends, God was often called by the ancient title, El

God's response to Job is built on the issues of the Creator's power and nurturing care.

	Speech 1 (38:1–40:2)	**Speech 2** (40:6–41:26)
Challenge	Who are you (38:2-3)?	Are you more just than I (40:7-8)?
Questions	Can you take care of the world (38:3–39:30)?	How great is your power over evil and chaos (40:9–41:26)?
Job's response	I will keep still (40:3-5).	I acknowledge the wonder of your creative power and care; I thank you for appearing to me and entrust myself to you (42:2-6).

Shaddai, translated by the NABRE with the traditional "the Almighty." The name Yahweh reveals the God of the storm to be the God of Israel's story, even though the book's characters are foreigners and the book makes no clear reference to historical events.

Although the primary speaker in the storm is the Lord, Job also speaks to create a form of dialogue between them (40:3-5 and 42:1-6). These speeches appear in the book as one more set of arguments in the debate, yet their climactic position and the divine authority of the main speaker grant them significance beyond the others. Carefully structured thematically, they progress through the creation of the cosmos to the wonders of the animal world, and then concentrate on particular animals called Behemoth and Leviathan.

38:1–40:2	Creation of the cosmos and its non-human inhabitants
40:3-5	Job's silence
40:6–41:26	Creation of Behemoth and Leviathan
42:1-6	Job's Enigmatic Response

These speeches are as puzzling as they are beautiful. A major interpretive question of the book is how the speeches relate to what precedes and follows them. To this point, the major question of the debate has been why Job suffers, and thus far, no consensus has emerged among the speakers. Readers might, therefore, expect God to settle matters between Job and his friends. Instead, God changes the subject, interrogating Job about his knowledge of creation. Equally puzzling are Job's responses to God's words. In his first response, he silences himself; in the second, he ignores his promise not to speak again, and the words he speaks are ambiguous.

Another interpretive issue regarding events in the storm is how to understand God's questioning of Job. Do God's questions disrespect or belittle Job and his suffering? Is God introducing new themes to set Job's suffering in a different perspective? Some scholars

and shown the dawn its place
13For taking hold of the ends of the earth,
till the wicked are shaken from it?
14The earth is changed as clay by the seal,
and dyed like a garment;
15But from the wicked their light is withheld,
and the arm of pride is shattered.
16Have you entered into the sources of the sea,
or walked about on the bottom of the deep?
17Have the gates of death been shown to you,
or have you seen the gates of darkness?
18Have you comprehended the breadth of the earth?
Tell me, if you know it all.
19What is the way to the dwelling of light,
and darkness—where is its place?
20That you may take it to its territory
and know the paths to its home?
21You know, because you were born then,
and the number of your days is great!
22Have you entered the storehouses of the snow,
and seen the storehouses of the hail

continue

The Lord Answering Job Out of the Whirlwind (38:1), William Blake

[23]Which I have reserved for times of distress,
for a day of war and battle?
[24]What is the way to the parting of the winds,
where the east wind spreads over the earth?
[25]Who has laid out a channel for the downpour
and a path for the thunderstorm
[26]To bring rain to uninhabited land,
the unpeopled wilderness;
[27]To drench the desolate wasteland
till the desert blooms with verdure?
[28]Has the rain a father?
Who has begotten the drops of dew?
[29]Out of whose womb comes the ice,
and who gives the hoarfrost its birth in the skies,
[30]When the waters lie covered as though with stone
that holds captive the surface of the deep?
[31]Have you tied cords to the Pleiades,
or loosened the bonds of Orion?
[32]Can you bring forth the Mazzaroth in their season,
or guide the Bear with her children?
[33]Do you know the ordinances of the heavens;
can you put into effect their plan on the earth?
[34]Can you raise your voice to the clouds,
for them to cover you with a deluge of waters?
[35]Can you send forth the lightnings on their way,
so that they say to you, "Here we are"?
[36]Who gives wisdom to the ibis,
and gives the rooster understanding?
[37]Who counts the clouds with wisdom?
Who tilts the water jars of heaven
[38]So that the dust of earth is fused into a mass
and its clods stick together?
[39]Do you hunt the prey for the lion
or appease the hunger of young lions,

continue

think the speeches portray God as a bully who uses superior knowledge and power to silence, shame, and overpower Job. In this view, God appears as the stronger one who out-talks Job the talker, and God disrespects and intimidates Job. But by attending to the poetic imagery of creation, the subject about which Job is ignorant, other interpretations are possible. Rather than doing battle with Job by means of the creation, God celebrates it in its beauty, wildness, and freedom. The speeches portray the breath-stopping creativity of God, the generative beauty of the cosmos and its inhabitants, and the wild freedom of God's creatures. This experience transforms Job.

To grasp the power of these chapters, it is best not to think of God's words as didactic answers to Job's questioning, angry laments. Rather than prosaic instruction, these speeches are lyric poetry, hymn-like speeches, celebrating creation, the amazing web of life in its awesomeness and beauty. They describe what ecologists might call "the household of life," overflowing with energy and freedom. But, of course, readers wonder how these divine speeches relate to Job's suffering?

Together God's speeches form a thematic symmetry between Job's first outburst and events in the storm. Job himself introduced the subject of creation in the curse of his birth (3:1-26). There he tries to "uncreate" the cosmos, to turn day into night, light into darkness, and life into death. God replies to Job's rhetorical destruction of creation with rhetorical reconstruction and recreation. These questions re-establish the world from the bottom up, from the waters, to the stars, to the animal inhabitants.

The setting of the encounter is a tempest, a whirlwind or fierce storm (38:1). In the Old Testament storms are sometimes the setting for theophanies, that is, appearances of God to humans (Exod 19:16-20; 1 Kgs 19:11-13; Ps 18:7-17; Hab 3:14). Besides being a conventional place of divine-human encounter, the storm conveys divine power and mystery. But the storm also evokes Job's stormy life of suffering, as well as the deaths of his children who lost their lives in a "great wind" (1:19). Job meets

God face to face in the stormy chaos of his destroyed world, not in a safe haven protected from harm and tragedy. Finally, if the storm is not only the venue for God's appearance but also an aspect of revelation itself, then the storm implies a deity who is wild, beautiful, free, and deeply unsettling. The speeches do not explain suffering, but they do present Job's anguished sorrows as the place of divine encounter.

38:1–40:2 Yahweh's first speech

The many ambiguities of the divine speech begin in the introductory verses (38:1-3). God interrogates Job like an impatient judge speaking before a courtroom. Annoyance with Job appears to drive the first question. What does God mean by asking "Who is this who darkens counsel / with words of ignorance?" God surely knows who Job is, since God previously called him "my servant Job" (1:8; 2:3). Is this question a literary device by which God draws attention to Job's words? Could it be Elihu to whom these words refer? Is this a statement of divine impatience, or is it a testing of the character, as if to ask, "What are you made of, Job? Can you stand toe to toe with the Creator of the cosmos?" God then commands Job to prepare for battle by girding his loins. He calls Job by a Hebrew word, translated "man" in the NABRE, that means specifically a "man who is charged as military protector of women and children," that is, one ready for battle. Then God turns the tables to announce that it is now Job's place to be interrogated.

The subject of the interrogation is Job's knowledge of creation. Asking if Job knows who, where, and when, God picks up the creation theme Job introduced in his curse of his birth where he wanted to unmake God's creation of him (ch. 3). God depicts the cosmos as if it were a habitat, a large building for living creatures. Where was Job when God founded the earth? Does Job know its size, how it rests upon pedestals, or who placed its cornerstone? Was Job a witness when the morning stars sang like a choir? Of course, Job knows nothing about creation, nor can he reach back in memory to the beginnings of the world and the joyous chorus of stars that sang at creation. The ancients believed that the earth itself rested on pedestals and a great dome held the planets and the stars and separated the waters above from the waters below (Gen 1:6).

In a reimagining of the creation story (Gen 1:1–2:4), God asks about Job's knowledge of the sea (38:8-11), conceived as a newborn babe emerging from God's womb, dressed by

---

40 While they crouch in their dens,
or lie in ambush in the thicket?
41 Who provides nourishment for the raven
when its young cry out to God,
wandering about without food?

CHAPTER 39

1 Do you know when mountain goats are born,
or watch for the birth pangs of deer,
2 Number the months that they must fulfill,
or know when they give birth,
3 When they crouch down and drop their young,
when they deliver their progeny?
4 Their offspring thrive and grow in the open,
they leave and do not return.
5 Who has given the wild donkey his freedom,
and who has loosed the wild ass from bonds?
6 I have made the wilderness his home
and the salt flats his dwelling.
7 He scoffs at the uproar of the city,
hears no shouts of a driver.
8 He ranges the mountains for pasture,
and seeks out every patch of green.
9 Will the wild ox consent to serve you,
or pass the nights at your manger?
10 Will you bind the wild ox with a rope in the furrow,
and will he plow the valleys after you?

continue

[11]Will you depend on him for his great
strength
and leave to him the fruits of your toil?
[12]Can you rely on him to bring in your grain
and gather in the yield of your threshing
floor?
[13]The wings of the ostrich flap away;
her plumage is lacking in feathers.
[14]When she abandons her eggs on the ground
and lets them warm in the sand,
[15]She forgets that a foot may crush them,
that the wild beasts may trample them;
[16]She cruelly disowns her young
and her labor is useless; she has no fear.
[17]For God has withheld wisdom from her
and given her no share in understanding.
[18]Yet when she spreads her wings high,
she laughs at a horse and rider.

continue

mother God in swaddling clothes of clouds and darkness, and kept within its limits like a baby in its playpen. From there God speaks of light (38:12-15), asking Job if he has commanded the day to begin and understands how the morning light changes the earth's appearance. Echoing the hymn to Wisdom (ch. 28), verses 16 and 17 attend to the sources of the sea, depths of the abyss, and gates of death.

In keeping with the often frightening imagery used to describe God's actions throughout the book of Job, when God finally comes to answer Job's charges, it is in the midst of a storm. If **God were to appear** to you in response to a prayer, what form do you think God would take? How do you imagine God would speak with you? Would you be intimidated by God's presence as Job appears to be, or would you be able to express your heartfelt thoughts and concerns with confidence?

These verses express ancient understandings of creation, its beginnings, the existence of the underworld, and sources of light, snow, hail, the winds, and the rain (38:22-38). With exquisite beauty, they set forth cosmic imagery of birth and nourishment. The heavenly constellations, in their mysterious appearances in each season (38:31-33), challenge Job's understanding of the rules governing heavenly bodies and his command of thunder and lightning. But Job is out of his depth. Only Wisdom was there with God at creation's beginning (Prov 8:22-36). God proudly points to each facet of the cosmos, showing it off to Job like a new homeowner delighting and bragging about their new home.

After God describes the wonders of the cosmic habitat, God interrogates Job about the inscrutable ways of its animal inhabitants (39:1-30). Equally beautiful and filled with the wild life-energy, diverse and unique, these creatures also confound Job. It is possible these animals come from royal lists of hunted animals and the icons that symbolized kings and their power. Some interpreters propose that these animals are negative in their association with wilderness and chaos, but if so, here they come firmly within divine control. Yet God's control of the earth and its animal inhabitants is not a subject of these speeches. Rather God appears to be bragging about the animals who occupy this magnificent habitat in their mysterious ways and stunning freedom. Regardless of the origins of this mixed list of creatures, each of them is beautiful, as well as joyously alive. With God's approval and expressive pride, each acts independently according to its own rhythms.

God's focus with the first three animals concerns the care and sustenance of their young (38:39–39:4). Lions, ravens, and mountain goats feed and give birth to their progeny. Does Job understand the various ways of birth in the animal world, each creature following its own times of gestation? The wild ass, the ox, and ostrich also live in freedom, resist human control, and act each according to their own kind (39:5-18). God has given the wild ass its freedom and gave it the wilderness for a home. Similarly, the wild ox cannot be bound with rope or domesticated to suit Job. Only the ostrich is subject to divine control, for the Creator has withheld wisdom from her. Yet even this ungainly animal is alive, making sport of horse and rider when she "spreads her wings high"; the ostrich is free and wondrous (39:18). The horse, too, is powerful and fearless, racing on the plains and into battle, while the eagle and the hawk elude human discernment and control (39:19-30).

God's depiction of the animals is one of pure delight in their variety, strength, and prowess. Job is a know-nothing in this arena. He cannot fathom the ways of his fellow creatures, in their assortment and inscrutability, and their freedom to grow and flourish in their dwelling places. In this first speech, God has expanded horizons of the debate from Job's suffering to the glories of the created world, a world characterized by beauty and energy of life.

Has God been bullying Job? Surely divine interrogation is terrifying and overwhelming. At the same time, God brings Job into a new frame of reference within which to view his own plight and to consider the way God relates to the world. Chapter 40 continues God's speech for two verses and ends with an intimidating question and a challenge that seems to say that God will brook no criticism from a "faultfinder" like Job.

40:3-5 Job's first response

Uncharacteristically, Job responds to God's speech by silencing himself. He announces that he is "of little account," a lightweight who has no answer to these many questions. Has he been cowed by an intimidating, interrogating God, or does his silence signify something more? Has he finally come to a place of wonder where he can step back and contemplate the beauty that has passed before him? Does his silence mean that he has become contemplative and now has room to come to grips with what he has lost and has been lamenting for many chapters? Perhaps his silence opens him, at last, to hear a response and to reframe his own

19Do you give the horse his strength,
and clothe his neck with a mane?
20Do you make him quiver like a locust,
while his thunderous snorting spreads
terror?
21He paws the valley, he rejoices in his strength,
and charges into battle.
22He laughs at fear and cannot be terrified;
he does not retreat from the sword.
23Around him rattles the quiver,
flashes the spear and the javelin.
24Frenzied and trembling he devours the
ground;
he does not hold back at the sound of the
trumpet;
25at the trumpet's call he cries, "Aha!"
Even from afar he scents the battle,
the roar of the officers and the shouting.
26Is it by your understanding that the hawk
soars,
that he spreads his wings toward the
south?
27Does the eagle fly up at your command
to build his nest up high?
28On a cliff he dwells and spends the night,
on the spur of cliff or fortress.
29From there he watches for his food;
his eyes behold it afar off.
30His young ones greedily drink blood;
where the slain are, there is he.

CHAPTER 40

1The LORD then answered Job and said:

2Will one who argues with the Almighty be
corrected?
Let him who would instruct God give
answer!

3Then Job answered the LORD and said:

4Look, I am of little account; what can I
answer you?
I put my hand over my mouth.
5I have spoken once, I will not reply;
twice, but I will do so no more.

continue

⁶Then the LORD answered Job out of the storm and said:

⁷Gird up your loins now, like a man.
I will question you, and you tell me the answers!
⁸Would you refuse to acknowledge my right?
Would you condemn me that you may be justified?
⁹Have you an arm like that of God,
or can you thunder with a voice like his?
¹⁰Adorn yourself with grandeur and majesty,
and clothe yourself with glory and splendor.
¹¹Let loose the fury of your wrath;
look at everyone who is proud and bring them down.
¹²Look at everyone who is proud, and humble them.
Tear down the wicked in their place,
¹³bury them in the dust together;
in the hidden world imprison them.
¹⁴Then will I too praise you,
for your own right hand can save you.
¹⁵Look at Behemoth, whom I made along with you,
who feeds on grass like an ox.
¹⁶See the strength in his loins,
the power in the sinews of his belly.
¹⁷He carries his tail like a cedar;
the sinews of his thighs are like cables.
¹⁸His bones are like tubes of bronze;
his limbs are like iron rods.
¹⁹He is the first of God's ways,
only his maker can approach him with a sword.
²⁰For the mountains bring him produce,
and all wild animals make sport there.
²¹Under lotus trees he lies,
in coverts of the reedy swamp.
²²The lotus trees cover him with their shade;
all about him are the poplars in the wadi.
²³If the river grows violent, he is not disturbed;

continue

experience. But the book, in its ambiguities and gaps, leaves interpretation to the readers, providing few clues to settle our many questions. No stage direction accompanies these speeches.

40:6–41:26 Yahweh's second speech

God's second speech repeats the opening challenge of the first (38:3) and amplifies it by asking Job if he would condemn God in order to justify himself (40:8). Although this challenge is indeed daunting, it does reveal that God has been listening to Job's accusations. God treats Job as a serious challenger, proposing that if Job can bring justice upon the earth by the power of his arm and the terror of his glance, then God would acknowledge that Job could save himself (40:9-13). Job, however, has not sought equality with God or the acquisition of power. He has been driven, instead, by a desire to understand his predicament.

After hurling this contest at Job as if he were a serious claimant to divine power, God turns to two specific and extremely frightening animals to further interrogate him. The first

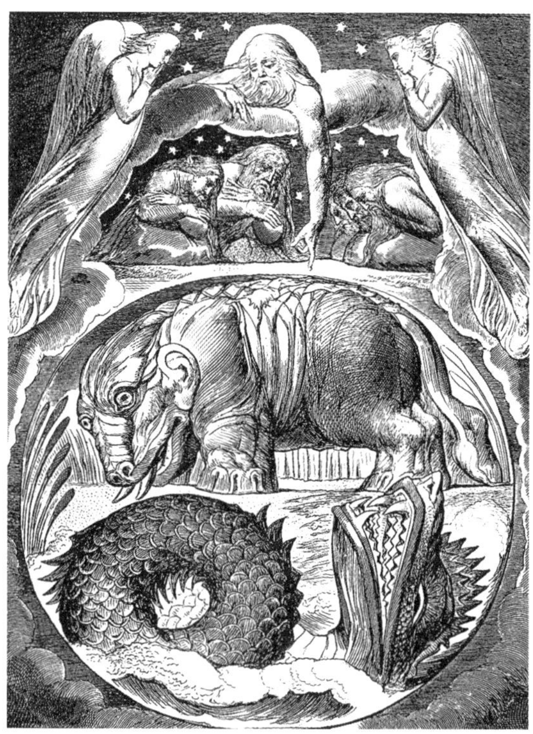

Behemoth and Leviathan (40:15, 25), William Blake

creature, Behemoth, is a land monster (40:15-24), and the second, Leviathan, is a sea monster (40:25–41:26). Some interpreters think Behemoth and Leviathan represent the hippopotamus and the crocodile, but it is more likely that they are mythic creatures who symbolize primordial chaos that God overcame at the creation of the world. They may be examples of the wicked ones that God challenges Job to "tear down the wicked in their place" (40:12). But God's relationship with these creatures is not adversarial; it is full of boastful pride.

The first statement about Behemoth addresses Job directly and asserts Behemoth's creaturely equality with Job. "Look at Behemoth, whom I made along with you" (40:15). An animal of marshy waters, Behemoth is far stronger than Job, but both are creatures of God. Stiff-tailed and iron-boned, Behemoth is wild, ferocious, and makes sport of other wild animals (40:20). He is not disturbed by turbulence, and no one can capture him in his idyllic domain that provides for all his needs. Job and he are equals in God's creation.

The Leviathan (40:26–41:26) is an even more fearsome creature. Job has already mentioned this monster twice: once, in his opening speech, when he wishes "those skilled at disturbing Leviathan" to curse the night of his conception (3:8), and again, when Job asks if he must be watched like the sea monster for being chaotic and uncontrollable (7:12). Now God brings that beast before Job for his reflection, perhaps as a kind of mirror. Again God brags about the power, strength, and awesome beauty of this creature. Again interpreters see here evidence of ancient Ugaritic creation myths where God does battle with chaos monsters. But although those traditions are probably present, they are greatly tamed in this speech, since a battle does not occur.

God asks Job if he can curb, tame, domesticate, or do battle with this creature (40:25-32). Job must answer God's question with a resounding "No!" He cannot control this creature, but neither does God claim to do so. Instead, God shifts from questioning Job to a stance of ebullient delight in the wondrous Leviathan

he is tranquil though the Jordan surges
about his mouth.
24 Who can capture him by his eyes,
or pierce his nose with a trap?
25 Can you lead Leviathan about with a hook,
or tie down his tongue with a rope?
26 Can you put a ring into his nose,
or pierce through his cheek with a gaff?
27 Will he then plead with you, time after
time,
or address you with tender words?
28 Will he make a covenant with you
that you may have him as a slave forever?
29 Can you play with him, as with a bird?
Can you tie him up for your little girls?
30 Will the traders bargain for him?
Will the merchants divide him up?
31 Can you fill his hide with barbs,
or his head with fish spears?
32 Once you but lay a hand upon him,
no need to recall any other conflict!

CHAPTER 41

1 Whoever might vainly hope to do so
need only see him to be overthrown.
2 No one is fierce enough to arouse him;
who then dares stand before me?
3 Whoever has assailed me, I will pay back—
Everything under the heavens is mine.
4 I need hardly mention his limbs,
his strength, and the fitness of his
equipment.
5 Who can strip off his outer garment,
or penetrate his double armor?
6 Who can force open the doors of his face,
close to his terrible teeth?
7 Rows of scales are on his back,
tightly sealed together;
8 They are fitted so close to each other
that no air can come between them;
9 So joined to one another
that they hold fast and cannot be parted.
10 When he sneezes, light flashes forth;
his eyes are like the eyelids of the dawn.

continue

[11]Out of his mouth go forth torches;
sparks of fire leap forth.
[12]From his nostrils comes smoke
as from a seething pot or bowl.
[13]His breath sets coals afire;
a flame comes from his mouth.
[14]Strength abides in his neck,
and power leaps before him.
[15]The folds of his flesh stick together,
it is cast over him and immovable.
[16]His heart is cast as hard as stone;
cast as the lower millstone.
[17]When he rises up, the gods are afraid;
when he crashes down, they fall back.
[18]Should a sword reach him, it will not avail;
nor will spear, dart, or javelin.
[19]He regards iron as chaff,
and bronze as rotten wood.
[20]No arrow will put him to flight;
slingstones used against him are but
straw.
[21]Clubs he regards as straw;
he laughs at the crash of the spear.
[22]Under him are sharp pottery fragments,
spreading a threshing sledge upon the
mire.
[23]He makes the depths boil like a pot;
he makes the sea like a perfume bottle.
[24]Behind him he leaves a shining path;
you would think the deep had white hair.
[25]Upon the earth there is none like him,
he was made fearless.
[26]He looks over all who are haughty,
he is king over all proud beasts.

CHAPTER 42

[1]Then Job answered the LORD and said:

[2]I know that you can do all things,
and that no purpose of yours can be
hindered.
[3]"Who is this who obscures counsel with
ignorance?"

continue

(41:2-26). In the style of a hymn of praise, God praises Leviathan's fierceness, his strong limbs, terrible teeth, scales on his back, fire from his nostrils, and his general imperviousness to attack. Even the "gods" are afraid when this creature rises up from the sea (41:17). "Upon the earth there is none like him" and "he is king over all proud beasts" (41:25-26). Although Leviathan is a fierce, proud creature suited for combat, this poetry is not about warfare between God and the wild creature. It is about divine joy in this most intrepid and fearsome animal. God does not repress Leviathan and Behemoth nor act in hostility toward them. Instead, the Creator leaves them in their natural state, uncontrolled and free to be themselves, wild and beautiful.

Rather than waging war with the creatures or even with Job, God opens up before Job the panorama of creation in its energy, variety, and wild beauty. Surely Job would be in fear and awe before this display, yet something more than intimidation is at work here. In the midst of the storm, God draws Job's attention away from himself to the awesomeness of the cosmos and its residents, kin to him, fellow creatures, untamed, and following their own paths. Some scholars note the absence of human creatures from God's speeches, yet humans are present in Job who is the one whom God addresses. God shows Job a world of immense marvels and beauty. Job participates in this glorious world and is one with it. This changes everything.

42:1-6 Job's second response

Job's final response reveals that his experience in the storm satisfies him and transforms his life, even if his words leave interpreters in doubt. Although Job promised previously to remain silent, he speaks again, acknowledging God's sovereignty and unstoppable will (42:2). Humbly he declares his know-nothing status before the glories of God's unfathomable creation. And he testifies that his encounter with God has altered him, as if he has become happily content with the experience of mystery and made alive again.

Job used to know about God through the words of other people, "by hearsay," but now in a marvelous declaration, he claims, "my eye has seen you" (42:5). Such seeing may refer to a vision, a common means of revelation in the Old Testament, but surely it signifies more. Job evokes Jeremiah's famous passage where the new covenant will mean that people will no longer teach one another because "Everyone, from least to greatest, shall know me" (Jer 31:34). Job is no longer reliant upon the word of others to have connection with God. Now he knows God directly from his own experience. With his own eye, in his own body, he has met God face to face.

The last line of his response, however, complicates interpretation of Job's words. Traditionally translated, "Therefore I despise myself and repent in dust and ashes" (42:6), the verse actually allows for several translations. In the NABRE translation, Job disowns his words and repents even though he is a righteous man. Both translations create problems. The former leaves Job in self-hatred, a defeated man beaten down by God. The latter shows Job renouncing the truthful laments he has set before God, who, in turn, praises Job's speech in the epilogue (42:7). But the Hebrew word often translated "repent" can also mean "be comforted," or "regret." Other translations create different nuances. In one, Job retracts his words and "is comforted by dust and ashes." In another, Job "rejects" the "dust and ashes," meaning that Job has stopped grieving and gotten on with his life.

The ambiguities of this line resist oversimplification. In light of the book's puzzling structure and unresolved debate, it is likely that the ambiguity is deliberate, a means to invite readers to enter Job's experience and come to terms with it for themselves. Whereas many interpreters find the speeches in the storm to be marked by chaos that Job learns to accept, this commentary concentrates the beauty of both the language and events in the storm. The breathtaking attraction of God's creation draws Job in and transforms him. The beauty of God and God's world allures, takes him outward from his suffering, and enables him to relinquish his imaginary position at the center of the world. Experience of beauty

I have spoken but did not understand;
things too marvelous for me, which I did not know.
4"Listen, and I will speak;
I will question you, and you tell me the answers."
5By hearsay I had heard of you,
but now my eye has seen you.
6Therefore I disown what I have said,
and repent in dust and ashes.

IX. Epilogue

Job's Restoration

7And after the LORD had spoken these words to Job, the LORD said to Eliphaz the Temanite, "My anger blazes against you and your two friends! You have not spoken rightly concerning me, as has my servant Job. 8So now take seven bulls and seven rams, and go to my servant Job, and sacrifice a burnt offering for yourselves, and let my servant Job pray for you. To him I will show favor, and not

continue

sharpens attentiveness, creates a contemplative spirit, provokes gratitude, and opens one to care for the world.

Job's long, angry laments have helped to heal him and opened him to the life-affirming greeting from God. However we deal with the many lingering puzzles of the book, its beauty points to the beauty of the Creator and summons readers to the possibility of encounter with God in any of life's circumstances.

EPILOGUE

Job 42:7-17

The book surprises readers again by returning in a short epilogue of ten verses to prose narrative. These verses not only resume the folktale genre of the prologue to form a narrative frame around the book, they also return to the worldview of the book's beginning. There

punish your folly, for you have not spoken rightly
concerning me, as has my servant Job." [9]Then Elip-
haz the Temanite, and Bildad the Shuhite, and
Zophar the Naamathite, went and did as the Lord
had commanded them. The Lord showed favor
to Job.
[10]The Lord also restored the prosperity of Job,
after he had prayed for his friends; the Lord even
gave to Job twice as much as he had before. [11]Then
all his brothers and sisters came to him, and all
his former acquaintances, and they dined with
him in his house. They consoled and comforted
him for all the evil the Lord had brought upon
him, and each one gave him a piece of money and
a gold ring.
[12]Thus the Lord blessed the later days of Job
more than his earlier ones. Now he had fourteen
thousand sheep, six thousand camels, a thousand
yoke of oxen, and a thousand she-donkeys. [13]He
also had seven sons and three daughters: [14]the first
daughter he called Jemimah, the second Keziah,
and the third Keren-happuch. [15]In all the land no
other women were as beautiful as the daughters
of Job; and their father gave them an inheritance
among their brothers.
[16]After this, Job lived a hundred and forty
years; and he saw his children, his grandchildren,
and even his great-grandchildren. [17]Then Job
died, old and full of years.

coherent themes of cause and effect rule in contrast to the poetry where ambiguity, complexity, and contradiction dominate the debates. The epilogue adds further complications to the book, even as it provides a satisfying happy ending. It brings readers back to a life where the good are rewarded and the wicked punished, as if the anguishing debates about God and human suffering only lead back to the beginning, having achieved little. The epilogue divides into two scenes: Job and friends (42:7-9) and Job's new life (42:10-17).

42:7-9 Job and friends

The narrator connects the epilogue with the speeches in the storm by setting events immediately "after the Lord had spoken these words to Job" (42:7). In these verses, God finally grants what Job desired all along, vindication of his righteousness or, at least, of the righteousness of his speech. But this honoring of Job's words is indirect, for it occurs in speech addressed to Eliphaz and comes only after God rebukes the friends, for "You have not spoken rightly concerning me, as has my servant Job" (42:7). It is strange that God does not affirm Job's words in the storm nor affirm him directly here. It may be that when Job sees God with his eye his needs are met and there are no other requirements of healing gestures between them.

The epilogue does not re-impose the theology of the prologue completely. Although the epilogue rewards Job, the innocent one, God does not punish the friends, so the chain of cause and effect is broken. God sets in place dynamics for rebuilding the friendship that fell upon the rocks of their disputes about Job's suffering. God tells Eliphaz and his two friends to offer sacrifice and Job will pray for them. God will not punish them because of Job's prayer. Job's experience of God in the storm enables him to intercede on his friends' behalf, altering his relationship with them and effecting a renewal of community. Job, the victim, extends a gesture of reconciliation to his persecuting friends.

42:10-17 Job's new life

God does more than approve of Job's words. In the second scene, God rewards him with good things, returning once again to the theology of the prologue. Job never asked God for restoration of anything he had lost except for their relationship. Now that Job has seen God himself, God gives him double what he had before (42:10-12). Among the doublings, Job's community comes first. Friends and family gather around him, feast with him, present gifts, and offer genuine comfort, "for all the evil the Lord had brought upon him" (42:11). Then he receives doubled numbers of animals and material wealth to make him twice as rich as before.

It is probably mistaken to ask where this community has been all along, since folktales tell their stories for the sake of the narrated events rather than to raise unanswered questions. Similarly, the replication of his family of ten children in the same gender balance as before does not address what all parents know, that lost children can never be replaced by new ones. The new children signify, instead, that Job has a full life, replete with a large family. But even this blessing is in some ways altered from the prologue because Job's daughters are not only named, they are given an inheritance with their brothers. By naming the daughters, and even more strikingly, listing them among inheritors, Job acts in ways his culture would find suspect (but see Num 27:1-11). Here the daughter's inheritance underscores Job's vast wealth as sufficient to include them, and for modern readers, it suggests that Job is not bound by the usual constraints of his society.

Job, the blessed servant of Yahweh, has come full circle. Restored to health, wealth, and community, he lives to see his children's children and dies old and full of years. And his latter days were more blessed than the former (42:12). Is this as a reward for his innocence, or is it a case of God pouring forth grace upon the beloved?

God declares that Job, who has challenged God and demanded vindication throughout the book, **has spoken rightly**, whereas the friends, who have praised God and defended God's justice, have not. The friends will only be forgiven if Job prays for them. Why? No answer is given. However, Job is the only person who speaks *to* God after chapter 2; the friends only talk *about* God. Job speaks honestly from his own experience, whereas the friends, who are not suffering, only parrot the traditional answers. God's vindication of Job is an affirmation of crying out to God in honest lament and trusting that God will answer.

CONCLUSION

The book of Job is too rich in meaning and metaphoric power and complex in literary structure and theological debate to be reduced to one interpretation. Here are some ways to reflect upon the book as a whole.

A dramatic process

From a literary perspective, the book of Job evokes experiences it is trying to express. The prologue positions readers as privileged interpreters, sympathizers with Job, because we know he is the innocent victim of a deal made in heaven. The seemingly endless debates between Job and his friends immerse us in Job's despair, the friends' frustration, and Job's rage at them and God. The book's spiraling, contradictory interchanges wear us down, as if it were designed to force us into the depth of the struggle, to wrestle with it, examine it from many sides, only to be surprised and unbalanced again by events in the whirlwind and epilogue.

Against Elihu's confident denial, God appears in the storm. With a literary beauty that replicates the beautiful wildness of creation itself, God draws Job and readers into a world beyond ourselves. There, no intellectual answers resolve the conflicting voices, but God and Job meet, and Job changes. Finally, we rest with Job in the epilogue, a rest foreshadowed by the hymn to wisdom (ch. 28). Although Job lives happily ever after in peace, many questions remain because Job, the righteous one, receives rewards.

Rather than restating orthodoxy or hammering home one interpretive viewpoint, the book implies that the hymn to wisdom is a key to interpretation. Humans can do many things, but wisdom is hidden to everyone but God, a point the book illustrates. By leaving unanswered questions, the book provokes active participation in the drama of Job's life from its collapse to its restoration. Such participation is potentially transformative for readers.

Innocent suffering

Rather than explain why the innocent suffer, the book spreads a feast of understandings

Job in Music, Art, and Literature

Poet Robert Frost

The book of Job has influenced countless artists, musicians, and writers, all of whom have created their own imaginative interpretations of this timeless Bible story. The British poet and artist William Blake (1757–1827) produced a series of engravings to illustrate Job (some of which are found throughout this book), while George Frideric Handel (1685–1759) set Job 19:25-26 ("I know that my Redeemer liveth, and that he shall stand at the latter day upon the earth. / And though worms destroy this body, yet in my flesh shall I see God.") to music as part of his famous oratorio *Messiah*. Perhaps the most provocative twentieth-century work dealing with Job is Robert Frost's "A Masque of Reason." Frost's poem, set centuries after the action of the biblical text, imagines a dialogue between Job and God, in which God explains that Job's trials were necessary if God were to be freed from "moral bondage to the human race." It was only after God had demonstrated by his treatment of Job that he was not constrained to always reward good and punish evil that God was set free to truly reign. The poem concludes with God awarding Job sainthood for his service as the "Emancipator of God."

and theological positions about the matter. In telling of Job's life it presents injustice, life-stopping losses, grief, and the collapse of the worlds. This narrative is capable of embracing the sufferings of individuals and of whole peoples. Rich Job loses all to join the poor and outcast, symbolized by his place on the ash heap or garbage dump of his village. This broken figure reappears in the homeless, frightened refugees, displaced persons, and the hungry millions of our rich world. Job's suffering is undeserved, and his friends further isolate him in their inability to see him as he really is. The book calls readers to face our responses to the suffering around us, near and far, and to note the suffering, like Job, are God's favored.

By undermining easy interpretations of Job's plight, the text reminds readers of the limited grasp on truth of our theological positions. Repeatedly, through structural juxtapositions of conflicting parts and voices, the book displaces each voice, interpretation, and point of view regarding Job's suffering. Such unsettling argument summons us to openness to other understandings, to humility in holding our own truth, and to recognition that theologies and spiritualities change with new human circumstances. In times of uncertainty and meaninglessness, Job also calls us to stubborn fidelity to the God who transcends all reduction to rigid and narrow doctrine.

The prologue presents Job's disaster as a calculated design made in a heavenly bargain. Job suffers physically, mentally, and spiritually. His friends believe Job sinned and God merely responded by punishing him. Job thinks God betrayed him and, by extension, treats the world unjustly. When God speaks, it is to change the subject from Job's suffering to the beauty and wild freedom of creation. The book does not explain Job's suffering, nor does any text of the Bible settle the matter. Rather than explaining suffering, the New Testament presents another One who suffers innocently and whose suffering and death on the cross culminates in the gift of new life.

God humbles Job

Another way to view the same literary evidence is to understand the book as a divine putdown of Job. Some interpreters believe that when God changes the subject from Job's suffering to the creation, God disrespects and abuses Job who complains for legitimate reasons. In this view, divine interrogation in the storm emphasizes God's power and humiliates Job. The book, therefore, conceives of divine-human relationship as continuing combat. Job curses and God overpowers, bullies, and silences Job. Job's second response, in the traditional, although disputed, translation, "I despise myself and repent in dust and ashes" (NRSV, 42:6), expresses Job's diminishment. God's attempt to restore Job's life shows Job's charges against God are correct. In this interpretive approach, the book reinstates divine power and keeps humans humbled in the chaos of life.

Divine-human relationship

The book's primary concern, however, may not be the suffering of the innocent but the larger question of human relationship to God in the midst of suffering. Job's catastrophe provides the flesh and blood mess within which to debate the character of divine-human relationship. The satan thinks divine-human relationship is a mercenary one. God buys human loyalty by giving gifts and putting a hedge of protection around Job. Job's words and actions in the prologue refute that point of view, for he remains utterly faithful. The satan disappears from the book because his role in the story is finished. He lost his bet.

Job's friends reverse the satan's perspective but are equally mechanistic. They insist that humans buy God's blessings or curses with their behavior. This theology of retribution gives humans controlling power over the actions of God. For both the friends and the satan, divine-human relationships are one-sided arrangements. The satan thinks God controls humans by giving or withholding good things. The friends think humans control God by loyalty or disloyalty. God has no choice but to bless or punish accordingly. Either way, divine-human relationship is compulsive and rule-driven.

Job breaks through these rigid patterns. In his experience, humans cannot control God, whom he finds to be both free and unreliable. He thinks God transcends human understanding, abides by no rules, and is inaccessible to humans. He thinks the sovereign God is beyond human capacity to understand and is also capricious and unjust. For him, God's being is deep mystery laced with cruelty.

When God appears, God not only affirms divine freedom, wildness, and beauty, but also the freedom and wild beauty of creation including Job. By implication, divine-human relationship is a mutual one where neither party controls the other, but both are free. In the epilogue, God approves Job's words. Is even Job's anger and despair about God's absence from the world evidence that Job has "spoken rightly" about God? (42:7). Are all Job's charges and accusations correct?

When God rejects the friends' words and declares Job to be right, the book appears to dismiss the friends' theology in the most authoritative way. But with great irony, the epilogue reinstates retribution. God blesses Job, the righteous one, and doubles all good things in his life. We are back where we started, but things are not the same.

Movement to mature faith

From another interpretative standpoint, Job's experiences resemble human struggles toward adult faith. As the story begins, Job is rich, secure, powerful, and surrounded by family and servants. Even when the satan removes his blessings, he remains righteous. His piety is precritical and unquestioning, and his life has clarity of purpose, driven by acceptance and trust.

But in the poetry, Job's trust evaporates as rage, doubt, and despair displace it. The collapse of his life brings with it loss of the traditions that had supported him. Formerly, he was a comforter of others and a leader among them. After the breaking of his world, his theology no longer holds. It cannot explain, support, or illuminate his life. Instead, his life challenges his theology. Adding to his pain, no new way of understanding emerges except his assumption that God has betrayed him. He faces what later contemplatives might call the "dark night of the soul," when all support for faith unravels and one plunges into divine absence.

Yet in the process, Job remains faithful. He grows in power and rhetorical expansiveness. He laments what he has lost, voicing his anger and grief to his friends and to God. His truthful, angry speech becomes a vehicle of his loyalty. Job holds fast to his integrity despite efforts of his friends to talk him out of his experience of the world. It enables him to dare to challenge God and to demand that God step forward and explain matters to him.

Job's life propels him from a faith of few challenges into a chaotic spiral of doubt where faith no longer has any buttress or external support. Yet in the midst of bitter strife, he never lets go of God. Instead, he cries and yells angrily at God, telling his truth and keeping their relationship alive. When Job and God meet in the storm, Job knows a "reorientation," a new way of being that exceeds doctrinal or philosophical answers. His encounter with the beauty of divine revelation, of the cosmos, and by implication, the beauty of God, provide him with direct spiritual experience and a sense of oneness with all life. He shares life with the Behemoth, the Leviathan—proud and joyous expressions of divine life. In the storm, Job glimpses a world energized by the creative power of God.

That glimpse of the absolute wondrousness of the Creator and of creation reorders his relationships. His communal life becomes more open, inclusive, and peaceful. He repairs friendships, interceding on behalf of his friends and extending extraordinary care to his daughters. In the storm, Job receives a life-affirming greeting from another world, and however we deal with the book's many lingering questions, its beauty calls us to glimpse God's amazing creativity divinely loosed in the cosmos. It summons us to care for creation and all its inhabitants, especially those who know Job's suffering and abysmal pain. It urges us toward lives of worshipful gratitude.

EXPLORING LESSON SIX

1. What is the basic structure of this final round of speeches (38:1–42:6)?

2. According to the commentary, what are two ways that God's intense questioning of Job has been interpreted?

3. In God's first speech, God does not directly respond to Job's accusations or self-defense (38:1–40:2). Instead, as the commentary explains, Job's "anguished sorrows" become "the place of divine encounter." Can you think of a time when you encountered God in the midst of great sorrow? What was the result of this encounter for you spiritually?

4. Are you surprised by Job's response to God's first speech (40:3-5)? Do you think Job is feeling intimidated or full of wonder? Embarrassed or inspired? Or a combination?

5. a) What is the effect on Job of God's second speech (40:6–41:26), where God glories in the wildness of creation, including even the fearsome creatures Behemoth and Leviathan (42:1-6)?

b) What might Job mean when he says he has "seen" God (42:5)?

6. The commentary discusses the difficulty posed by Job's final words to God: "Therefore I disown what I have said, / and repent in dust and ashes" (42:6). Reflecting on what the commentary says about this verse, as well as your own reading of Job, what do *you* think Job is expressing?

7. a) In the end, God is clear that Job's friends did not speak rightly about God, but Job did (42:7-8). What does this tell us about the traditional theology of retribution that Job's friends were so determined to defend?

b) How can this scenario help us reflect on our own theological certainties? How can we incorporate humility, human experience, and a more open-minded, open-hearted approach into our understanding of God's interaction with our world?

8. What was your initial reaction to the restoration of Job's health and wealth at the end of the book (42:7-17)? Did you find it satisfying, or did it raise additional questions for you?

9. The "Conclusion" section of the commentary explores several meaningful ways to reflect on the book of Job. What point in this section resonates most with you and why?

10. The book of Job honestly explores innocent suffering, but even more importantly, it explores how the divine-human relationship can endure through devastation and grief. What particular idea or insight about our relationship with God will you take with you from your study of Job?

CLOSING PRAYER

Prayer

Then the L*ORD answered Job out of the storm* . . . (Job 38:1)

Lord, you answered your servant Job out of a storm when his life was in chaos and he was nearly crushed by despair. Be with us, we pray, when we feel overwhelmed by the storms of misfortune in our lives. Let us always be comforted by your presence and the assurance of your love. We pray today for one another and for all those in need of your loving presence, especially . . .

PRAYING WITH YOUR GROUP

Because we know that the Bible allows us to hear God's voice, prayer provides the context for our study and sharing. By speaking and listening to God and each other, the discussion often grows to more deeply bond us to one another and to God.

At *the beginning and end of each lesson* simple prayers are provided for individual use, and also may be used within the group setting. Most of the closing prayers provided with each lesson relate directly to a theme from that lesson and encourage you to pray together for people and events in your local community.

Of course, there are many ways to center ourselves in God's presence as we gather together in groups around the word of God. We provide some additional suggestions here knowing you and your group will make prayer a priority as part of your gathering. These are simply alternative ways to pray if your group would like to try something different from those prayers provided in the previous pages.

Conversational Prayer

This form of prayer allows for the group members to pray in their own words in a way that is not intimidating. The group leader begins with Step One, inviting all to focus on the presence of Christ among them. After a few moments of quiet, the group leader invites anyone in the group to voice a prayer or two of thanksgiving; once that is complete, then anyone who has personal intentions may pray in their own words for their needs; finally, the group prays for the needs of others.

A suggested process:
In your own words, speak simple and short prayers to allow time for others to add their voices.

Focus on one "step" at a time, not worrying about praying for everything in your mental list at once.

Step One	Visualize Christ. Welcome him. Imagine him present with you in your group. Allow time for some silence.
Step Two	Gratitude opens our hearts. Use simple words such as, "Thank you, Lord, for . . ."
Step Three	Pray for your own needs knowing that others will pray with you. Be specific and honest. Use "I" and "me" language.

Step Four	Pray for others by name, with love. You may voice your agreement ("Yes, Lord"). End with gratitude for sharing concerns.

Praying Like Ignatius

St. Ignatius Loyola, whose life and ministry are the foundation of the Jesuit community, invites us to enter into Scripture texts in order to experience the scenes, especially scenes of the gospels or other narrative parts of Scripture. Simply put, this is a method of creatively imagining the scene, viewing it from the inside, and asking God to meet you there. Most often, this is a personal form of prayer, but in a group setting, some of its elements can be helpful if you allow time for this process.

A suggested process:

- Select a scene from the chapters in the particular lesson.
- Read that scene out loud in the group, followed by some quiet time.
- Ask group members to place themselves in the scene (as a character, or as an onlooker) so that they can imagine the emotions, responses, and thinking that may have taken place. Notice the details and the tone, and imagine the interaction with the Lord that is taking place.
- Share with the group any insights that came to you in this quiet imagining.
- Allow each person in the group to thank God for some insight and to pray about some request that may have surfaced.

Sacred Reading (or Lectio Divina)

This method of prayer invites us to "listen with the ear of the heart" as St. Benedict's rule would say. We listen to the words and the phrasing, asking God to speak to our innermost being. Again, this method of prayer is most often used in an individual setting but may also be used in an adapted way within a group.

A suggested process:

- Select a scene from the chapters in the particular lesson.
- Read the scene out loud in the group, perhaps two times.
- Ask group members to ponder a word or phrase that stands out to them.
- The group members could then simply speak the word or phrase as a kind of litany of what was meaningful for your group.
- Allow time for more silence to ponder the words that were heard, asking God to reveal to you what message you are meant to hear, how God is speaking to you.
- Follow up with spoken intentions at the close of this group time.

REFLECTING ON SCRIPTURE

Reading Scripture is an opportunity not simply to learn new information but to listen to God who loves you. Pray that the same Holy Spirit who guided the formation of Scripture will inspire you to correctly understand what you read, and empower you to make what you read a part of your life.

The inspired word of God contains layers of meaning. As you make your way through passages of Scripture, whether studying a book of the Bible or focusing on a biblical theme, you may find it helpful to ask yourself these four questions:

What does the Scripture passage say?
Read the passage slowly and reflectively. Become familiar with it. If the passage you are reading is a narrative, carefully observe the characters and the plot. Use your imagination to picture the scene or enter into it.

What does the Scripture passage mean?
Read the footnotes in your Bible and the commentary provided to help you understand what the sacred writers intended and what God wants to communicate by means of their words.

What does the Scripture passage mean to me?
Meditate on the passage. God's word is living and powerful. What is God saying to you? How does the Scripture passage apply to your life today?

What am I going to do about it?
Try to discover how God may be challenging you in this passage. An encounter with God contains a challenge to know God's will and follow it more closely in daily life. Ask the Holy Spirit to inspire not only your mind but your life with this living word.